CW01582686

The ultimate guide to Food Photography

Tips and tricks to take you from daunting to delicious

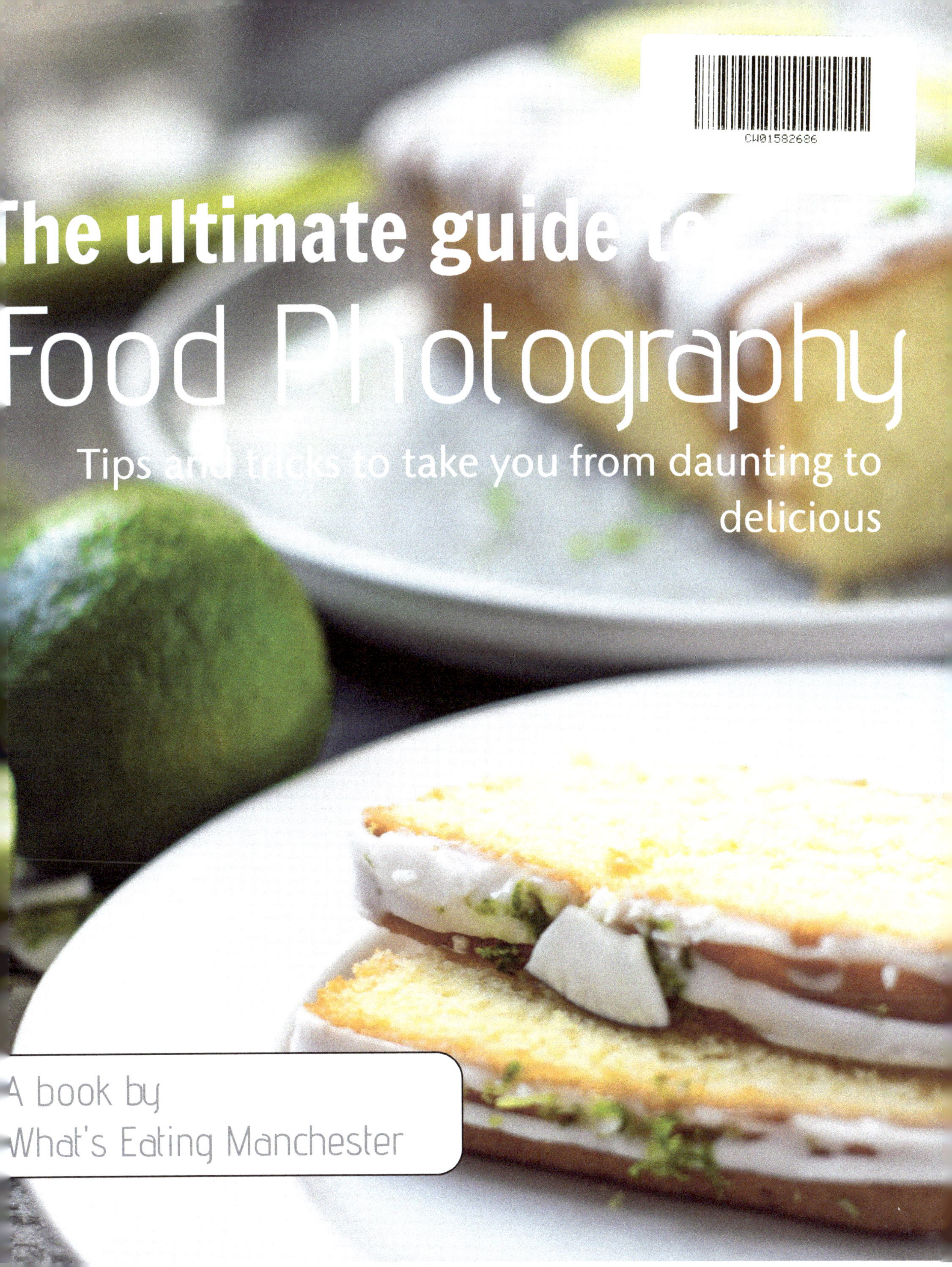

A book by
What's Eating Manchester

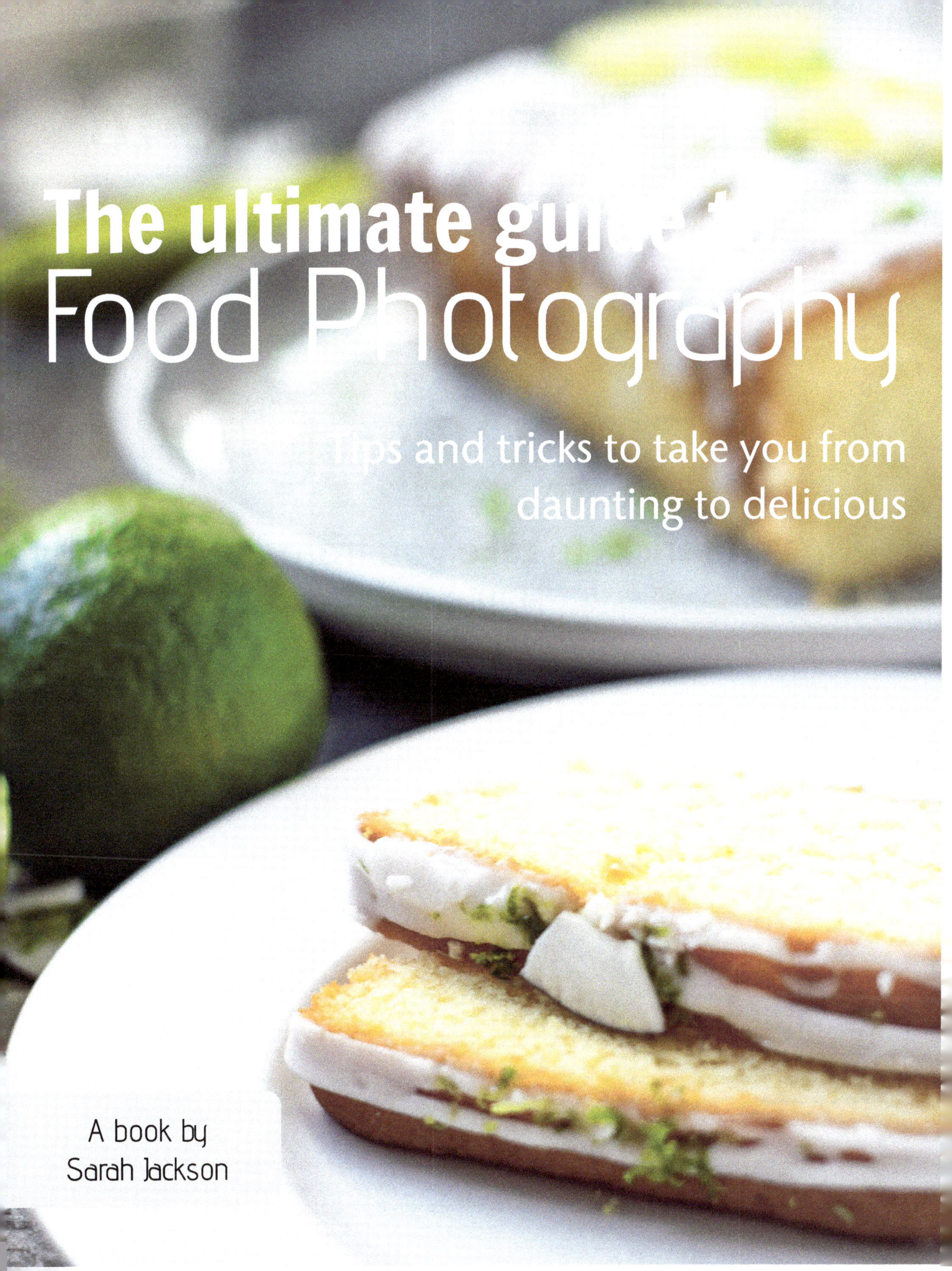

The ultimate guide to Food Photography

Tips and tricks to take you from daunting to delicious

A book by
Sarah Jackson

The ultimate guide to

Food Photography

Tips and tricks to take you from daunting to delicious

The Ultimate Guide to Food Photography

Sarah Jackson
whatseatingmanchester.com

Copyright © 2019 by Sarah Jackson

Notice of Rights
All rights reserved. No part of this book may be reproduced or transmitted in any form by any means, electronic, mechanical, photocopying, recording, or otherwise, without the prior written permission of the publisher.

Notice of Liability
The information in this book is distributed on an "As Is" basis, without warranty. While every precaution has been taken in the preparation of the book, the author shall have no liability to any per- son or entity with respect to any loss, damage, or injury caused or alleged to be caused directly or indirectly by the instructions contained in this book or by the computer software and hardware products described in it.

CONTENTS

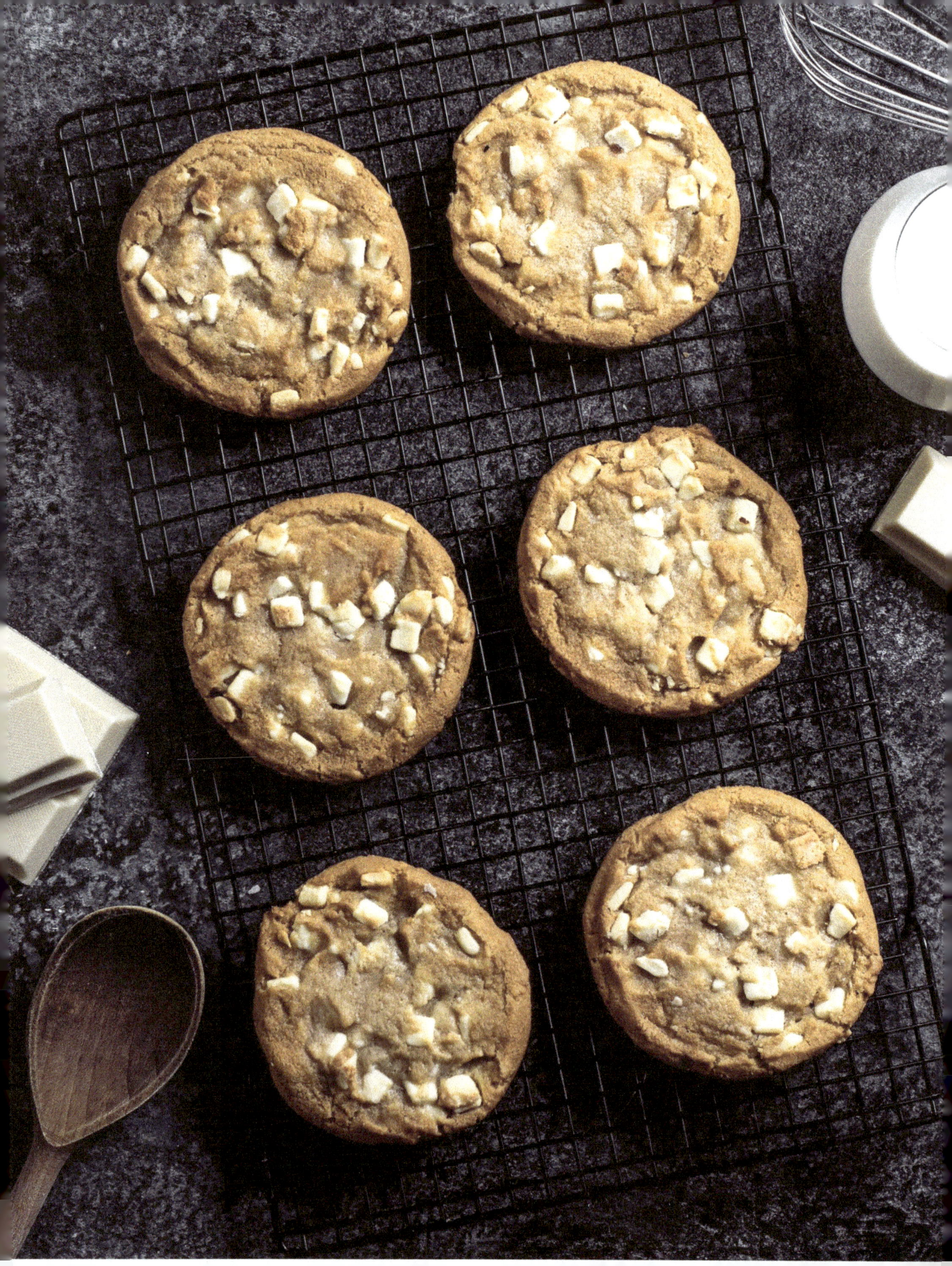

INTRODUCTION

With both photography and food being my passions for 10 years, it's only natural that despite my best efforts, I would fall head first into food photography. After being actively involved in the food photography blogging world for some time; I realized that unlike me, a lot of people who want to write about and photograph food, rarely came from a photography background. A closer look will prove this observation.

Clearly, not everyone knows about ISO and the difference between using a 50mm and a 200mm lens. This knowledge greatly helped me when I ventured to move into food photography and made the learning process so much easier. After this event, a desire to help other food bloggers that don't want to make a career out of being a food photographer, but just want to take beautiful images of food came alive in me.

This book is tailored to those of you who don't necessarily want to work for clients and have no resources to own a studio full of expensive equipment's, or a studio for that matter. It's for people who love food and want to acquire the basic knowledge of creating beautiful images.

So, whether you're a recipe blogger, a restaurant blogger, a chef or a cake maker. If you just want to take beautiful images of food, read on. I'll take you through the basics of food photography, how to use and where to source props, the best light, cameras, lenses, and everything in between.
We all have one common goal, to make beautiful food images. And I'm super excited for you to take this journey with me!

Tools for Digital Photography

Cameras

Food photography is not different from any other kind of photography. It still requires basic camera equipment, lighting, and a little know how. It's very important to have basic understanding of the fundamentals of photography before you take a leap into food photography. As a head start, understanding exposure, white balance, and basic composition will give you a solid foundation from which to build your food photography knowledge.

In this chapter, I will talk about the tools you will need, their basics, and usage.

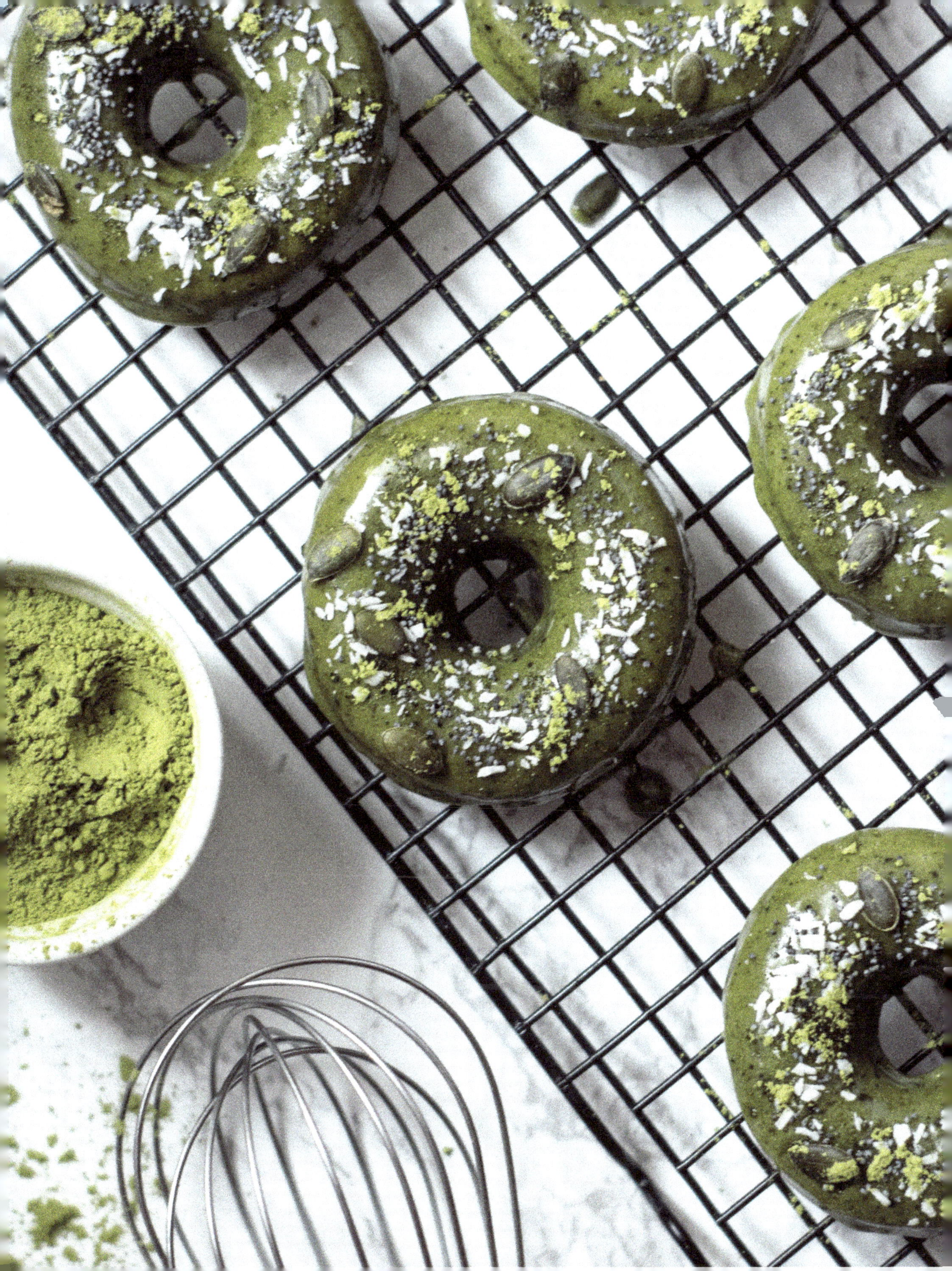

Digital Cameras

There are innumerable digital cameras in the market today and it can be difficult to successfully navigate through so many available options. Understanding the basics of different types of cameras will help you make informed decisions as to what's best for you. There are three types of camera on the market that we're going to go through today, point & shoot, DSLR, and mirror less.

Point & Shoot

Point and shoot cameras, as the name suggests, are cameras that allow you to just point, and shoot. They are greatly available on the market to count and your options in this category are almost limitless. Point and shoot cameras are good options for people just starting out, and have little or no knowledge of photography and just want the camera to do all the work except positioning.

With point and shoot cameras, you have a limited amount of creative freedom, mostly with the exception of bridge cameras; because, their exposure settings are set manually. Instead, you get to choose from a selection of pre-sets like, portrait, landscape or night mode. These pre-sets change the exposure setting of the camera to match the type of subject you are aiming or shooting.

This lack of freedom becomes problematic when you want to learn more about exposure and camera settings. With point and shoot cameras, you simply don't have the option to experiment. This is where I recommend a bridge camera. Mainly because they act as a bridge between a full DSLR and a point and shoot camera. Therefore, giving you the option of having some creative control, bridge cameras are my choice for absolute beginners. With most purchase, you can even get a very limited number of interchangeable lenses.

These types of camera will last longer than a point and shoot because you can grow and learn with them.

Point and shoot camera tip
If you already have a point and shoot camera and you're not quite ready to upgrade just yet. Try taking a photo of your food in portrait mode. Portrait mode usually gives you a lovely blurred background that is also excellent in food photography. Fake that shallow depth of field!

DSLR

DSLR stands for digital single-lens reflex. It is a professional-grade type of camera which uses a mirror behind the lens, which reflects the light up through a chamber and into the viewfinder, thus allowing you to see the subject. The three main advantages of a DSLR are their interchangeable lenses, creative freedom through customisable camera settings, and RAW capability. We'll get into RAW images a little later.

Interchangeable lenses, mirrorless, and DSLR cameras are a huge advantage. Having the freedom of tailoring your lens to a particular situation is an advantage that will only be experienced with a DSLR or mirrorless camera.

DSLR cameras offer an enormous amount of control with exposure and focal point. Offering the photographer, the option to control every aspect of the image making process.

Mirrorless

Mirrorless cameras don't have the mirror that DSLR cameras have. Hence the name mirrorless. Instead, it shows a digital representation of the subject in the viewfinder. This makes for a much smaller, and lighter camera. How the image is captured is not affected by this, so, there is very little difference between a DSLR and mirrorless camera in every other aspect.

Another advantage of DSLR and mirrorless cameras is their larger sensors, when compared to a point and shoot camera. There are two types of sensors available, a full frame or a crop; with both having their own advantages.

Crop sensor vs full frame

I won't go into too much detail about camera sensors because unless you are willing to shell out a few thousand dollars on your camera body, you're not likely to get a full frame camera. It is, however, important to understand that there is a difference and it is something you may want to take into account if you someday want to upgrade to a pro camera.

With a full frame camera, that is exactly what you will be seeing, the full frame. If you use a 200mm lens, what you will be seeing is 200mm view. With a crop sensor camera, you will see the picture in a cropped form. So, the image is larger, and magnified in the frame. If you were to use that same 200mm lens, you will see the equivalent of a 320mm lens.

When buying lenses, it's important to note that lenses that are designed to fit a full frame camera can be used with a crop sensor camera. However, the same cannot be said for the other way. Lenses designed for a crop sensor camera cannot be used with a full frame camera. So, when building your lens collection, you need to take this into account. If you plan on upgrading to a full frame camera in the future, you may want to consider buying lenses for a full frame.

So, which camera should I buy?

It's an age-old question, isn't it? Which camera should I buy? If you're just starting out, my recommendation would be a bridge camera, something that you can learn on and grow with.

If you have your heart set on a DSLR or mirrorless, setting a realistic budget and sticking with it would suffice. Most photographers will go through several camera bodies in their lifetimes, but will likely keep all of their lenses. I will personally opt for a cheaper camera body in order to afford a few different lenses.

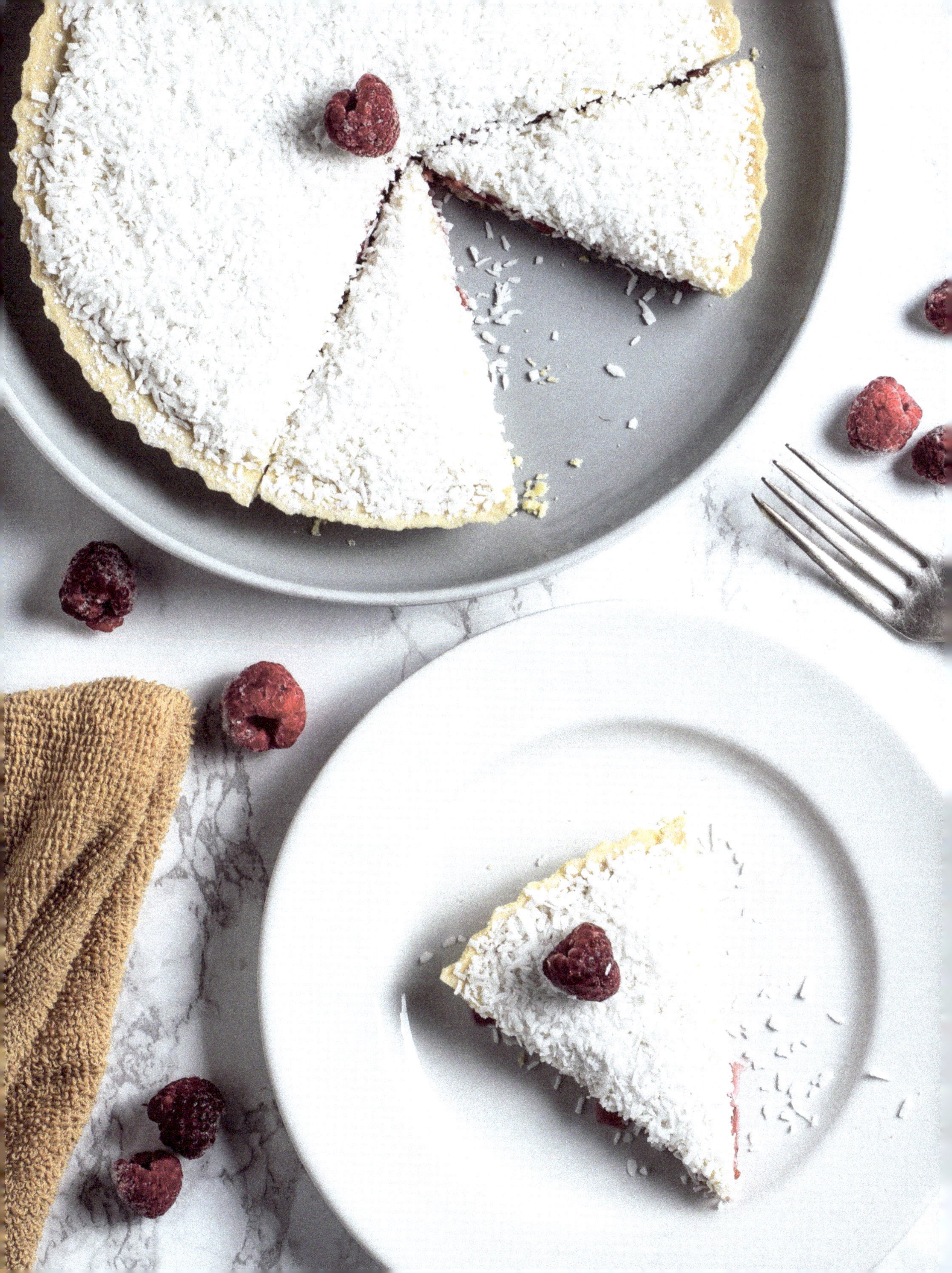

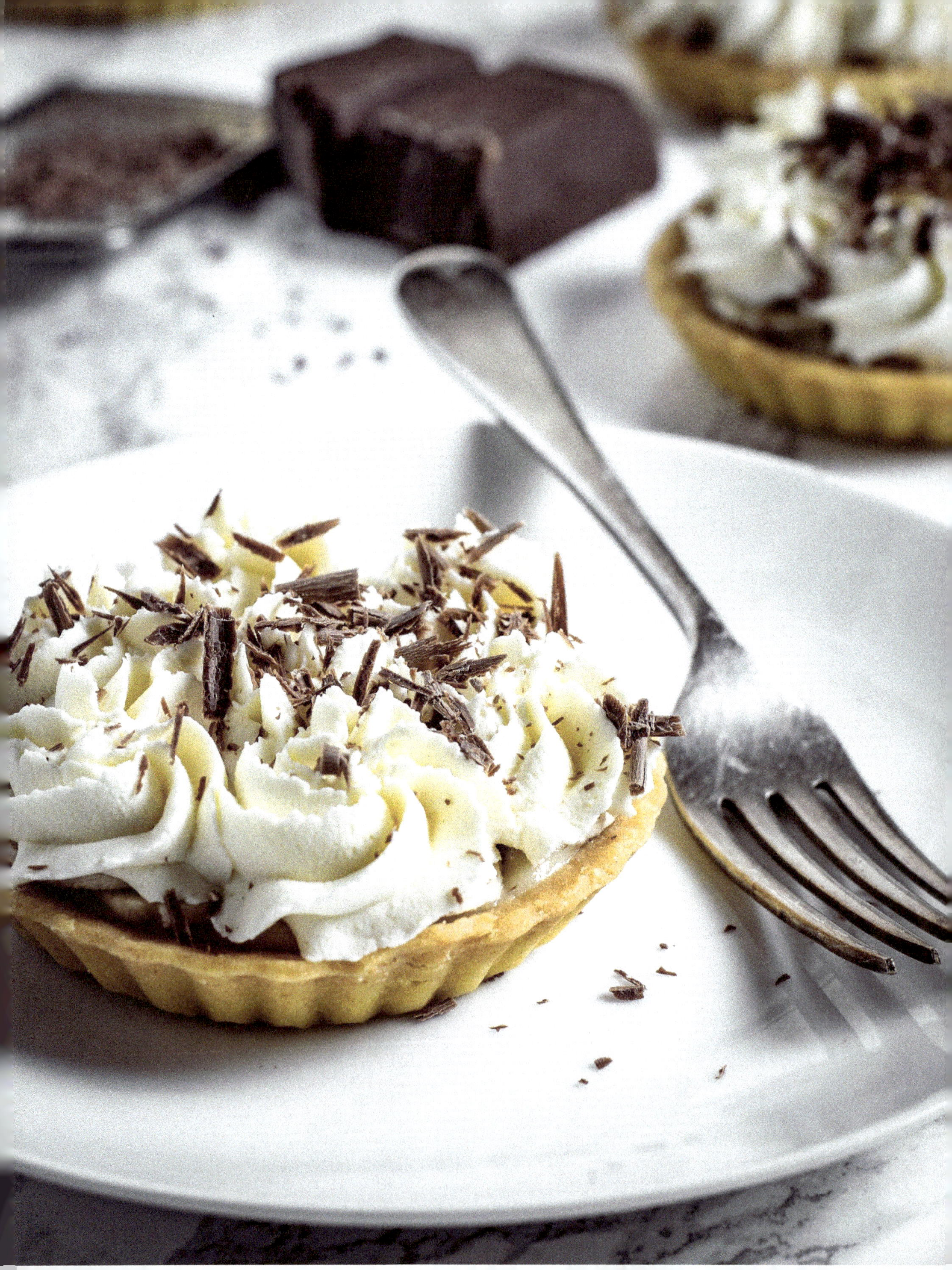

LENSES

Lenses and Focal Lengths

Lenses are the "eye" of the camera. Often considered the most important aspect of the camera, lenses come in a wide variety of focal lengths. Your choice of lens has a huge impact on the final image, determining the sharpness and the overall clarity.

The main types of focal length we are going to cover here are wide angle, mid-range, telephoto, and macro. Each of them do different jobs and play an integral role in a photographer's arsenal. However, realistically, as a food photographer, you may find yourself only using a macro or a mid-range lens.

Lenses help photographers to develop their own personal style. In a course of time, you might develop one or two lenses that you love and could hardly live without, therefore, you will reach for these lenses more often than others and they may help in developing your signature style.

Wide Angle

True to their name, wide angle lenses have a very wide-angle view. Used mostly in landscape photography to capture a vast landscape, they have a field of view from about 110 degrees to 60 degrees. A lens is considered wide angle from a focal length of 35mm or lower.

Most photographers don't use wide angle lenses for food photography because of a number of reasons. Firstly, the wider the lens, the more likely you will get distortion in your image. This distortion is not easily noticed with a vast landscape but is very jarring with a food image.

Wide angle lenses also have a greater depth of field. This means that it will be much harder and sometimes impossible to create that lovely blurred background that's favored with food images.

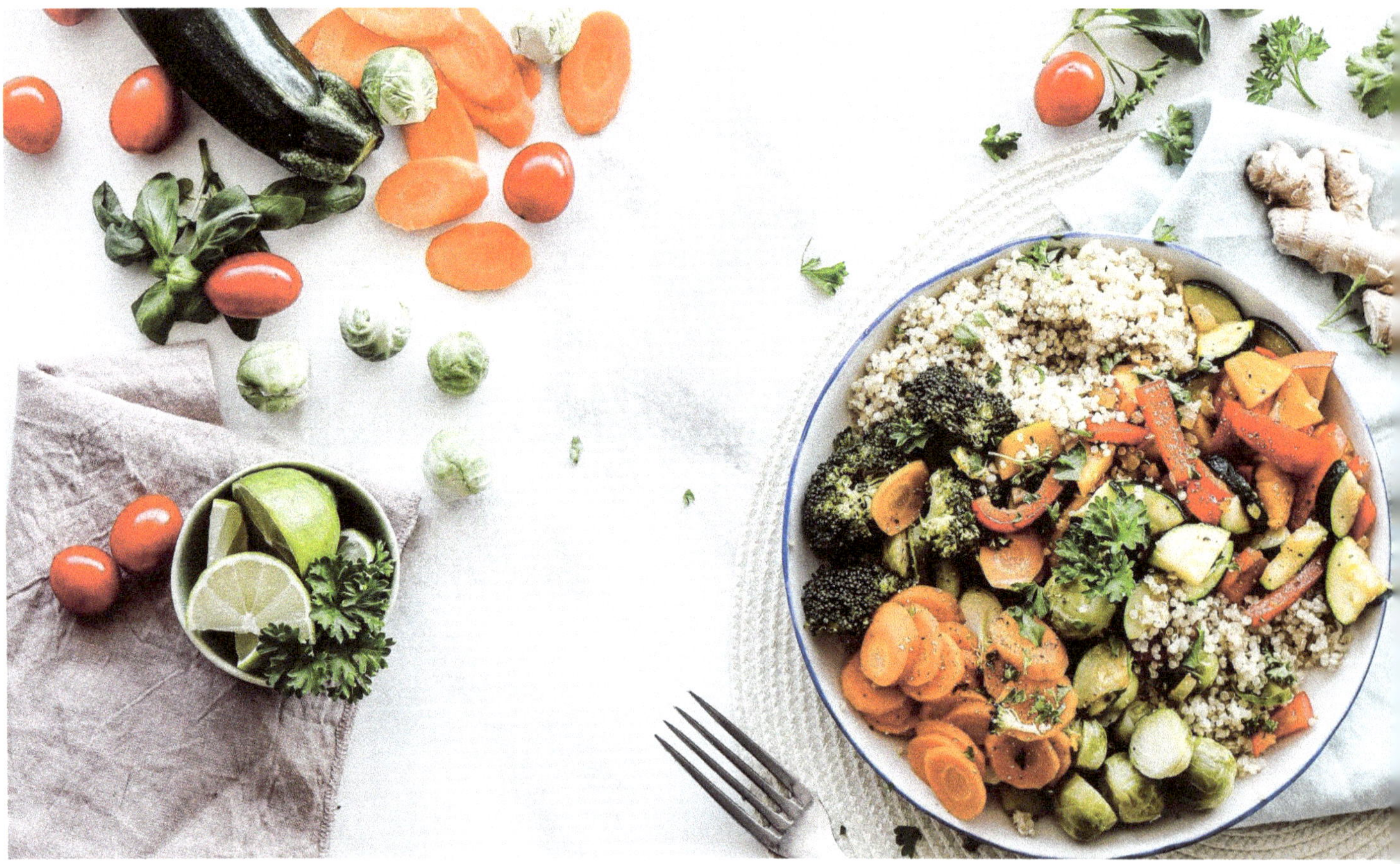

A wide-angle lens would be an appropriate option for an image like this as you need a wide field of view to capture all the scene and if you don't want to be on a ladder.

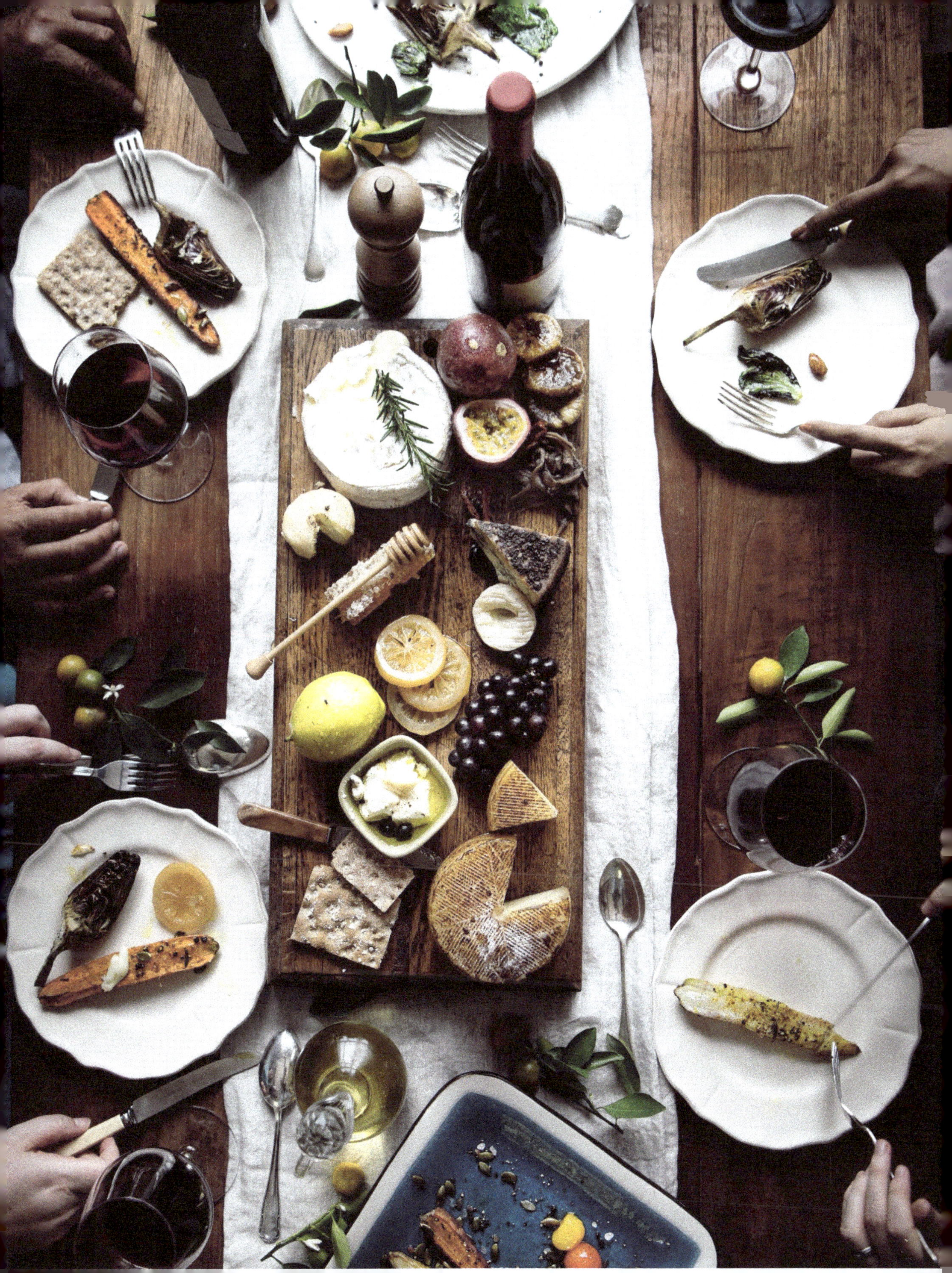

Mid-Range

Mid-range lenses generally have focal lengths between 35mm and 85mm. The perspective created with these lenses is very natural and produces very little distortion. With these lenses, it is possible to create a lovely shallow depth of field with an out of focus background that is popular with food images.

One of the most popular mid-range lenses for food images is a 50mm lens. You would be hard pushed to find a food photographer that doesn't have at least an inexpensive 50mm lens in their kit. This would be the lens I recommend to every beginner that wants to create beautiful food images.

Telephoto

Telephoto lenses are popular with nature, wedding and sports photographers for their ability to "zoom" into scenes and make seemingly distant objects appear closer.

Telephoto lenses start at around 100mm and go all the way up to 800mm and more. Obviously, with food images, unless you want to photograph a burger from across the street, you're not going to need anything close to 800mm.

If you're building your lens collection and looking to expand past the basics, a 105mm lens is a good option for food photography. It has a nice range and works great for portraits too if you ever need to photograph a chef or cook, this lens will have your back.

A 200mm lens is also a nice option for your kit. Photographing a food scene with a 200mm will create lovely compression making the background appear closer and giving you that great and authentic background blur.

Macro

There is often a misconception that macro lenses are reserved for nature photographers looking to get awesome images of ants. Macro lenses allow you to focus on objects very close to the camera. In food photography, this allows you to properly fill your frame when photographing smaller dishes.

When your subject is small, other lenses don't allow you to get close enough to properly fill your frame and get your subject in focus. With a macro lens, you don't need to pull away to get the subject in focus.

Moreover, with macro lenses, you can leverage getting close to your dish to photograph in detail.

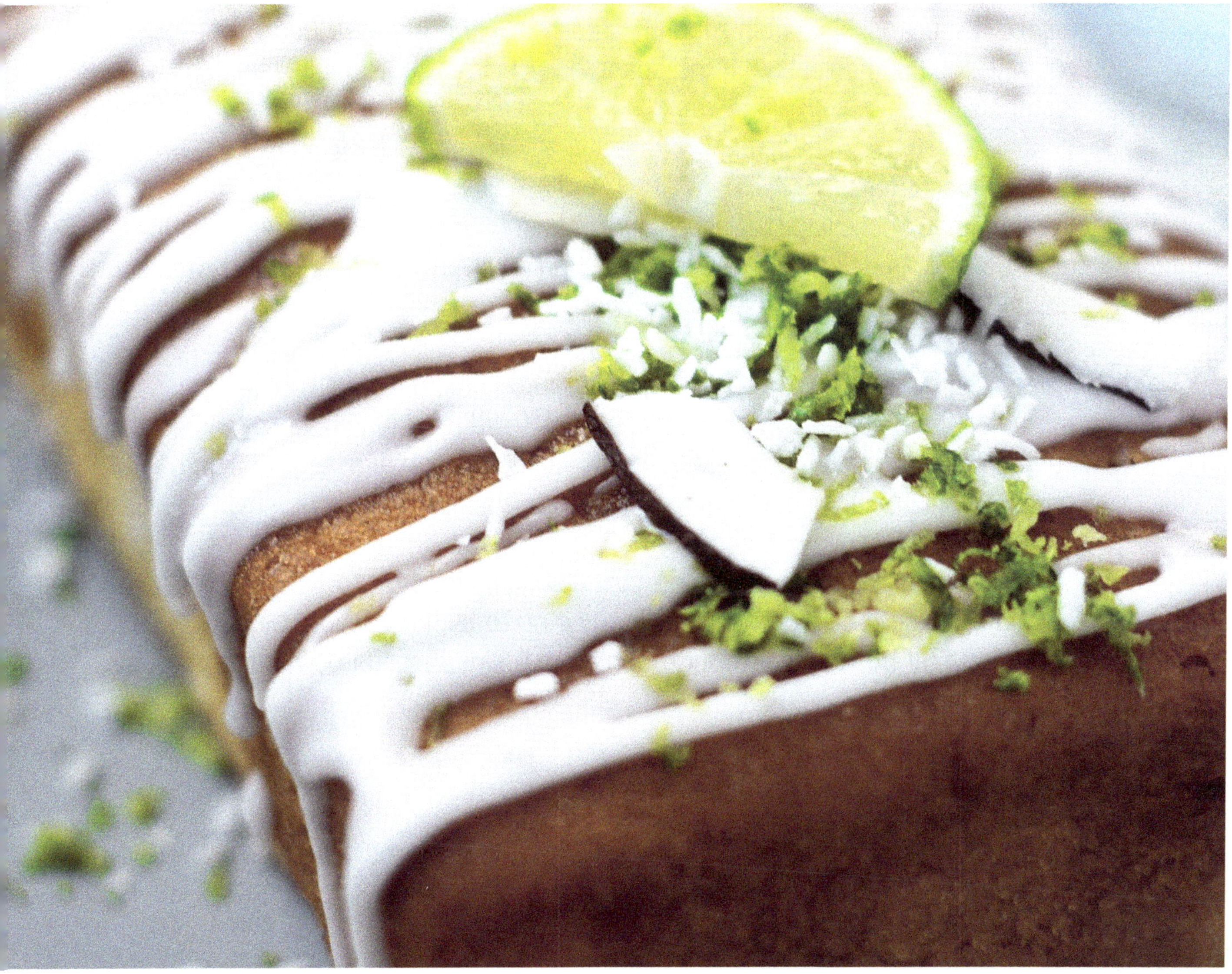

So, which lens should I buy?

This is a tricky question, and the answer is, whichever lens you want. But here are a few recommendations to think about.

50mm prime lens.
Often lovingly called the "nifty fifty" this lens will quickly become your go-to for everything. They are inexpensive, lightweight and will produce excellent results in most situations. Excellent if you want to shoot a flat lay overhead and capture a lot in the frame. Equally as good for capturing scenes at a 45-degree angle, often, these lenses have low aperture capabilities that will help you achieve that shallow depth of field.

24-105mm zoom lens.
Deploy these lenses for both food photography and portraits. If you're just starting out with food photography, I think spending your money on multi-function lenses is important.

100mm macro lens.
If you want a specialized lens for your food, you won't go wrong with a 100mm macro lens. This will let you fill an entire frame with your subject and get really close into its detail.

With these lenses, you really do get what you pay for. The quality of the glass makes all the difference. Prime lenses, that is fixed focal length lenses, will always be sharper and focus faster than a zoom. However, zoom lenses give you the option of either getting closer or further away from your subject.

When thinking about buying lenses, pick a budget and stick to it. Think about what you will photograph. Realistically, is food going to be the only thing you will ever photograph? If no, you may want to look into a lens that can do more than one job.

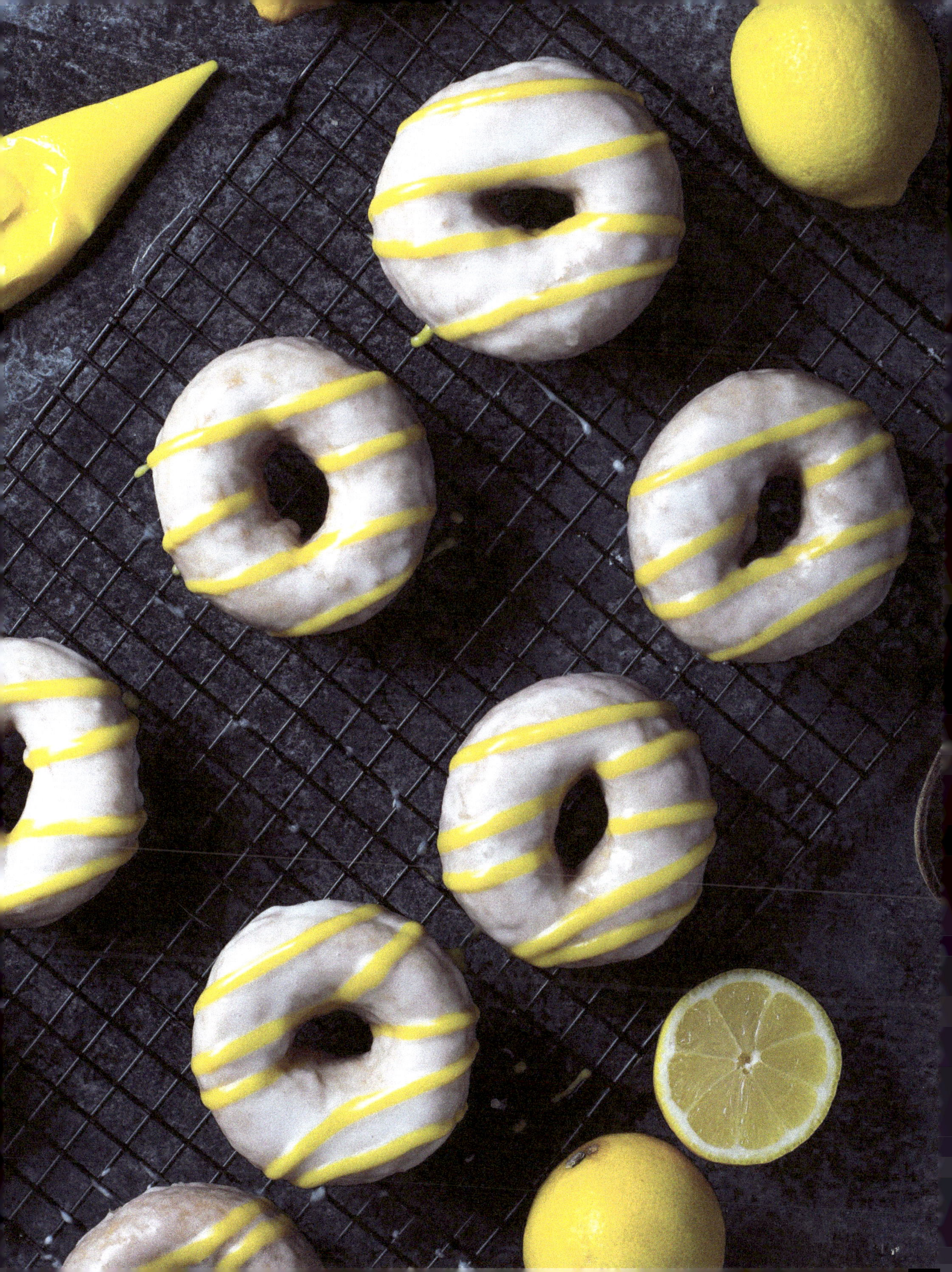

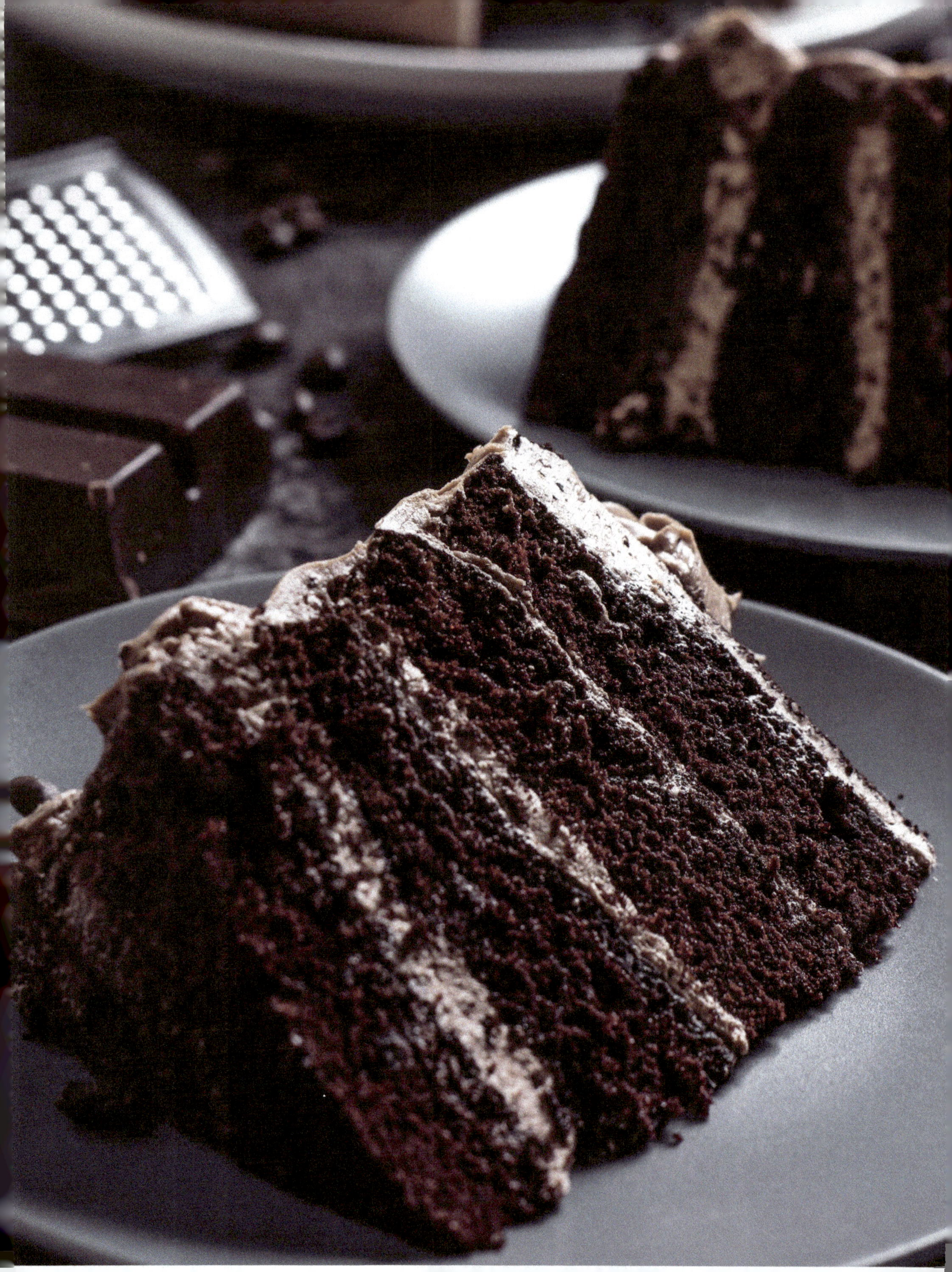

Tripods and Accessories

As with everything else in life, there are always those little extras that you don't necessarily need but will make your life a lot easier. With photography especially, you could spend a fortune buying accessories, so here are a few that you need to look into.

Tripods

Tripods come in many shapes and sizes. They are all made to do one thing, stabilize your camera. If you need to lower your aperture past around 1/80th of a second, you need to have something to hold your camera still.

When shopping for tripods, you need to think of how often you will be traveling with your tripod and how often you will need to lug it around. Generally, the heavier the tripod, the more stable it is. Studios often have huge, heavy tripods that even though they're on wheels, they take some real muscle to move around. On the other end of the spectrum, there are lightweight plastic tripods available that weigh next to nothing. These are made for photographers that need to move them around often and need to keep the weight down. The disadvantage of this is that a strong wind could result in a lot of damage to your camera.

You need to consider your needs and photograph. If you're only going to photograph food, I would recommend a tripod somewhere in the middle of the weight range. Something with either a flip out lateral arm or the ability to purchase this accessory separately. This is an arm that reaches out horizontally from the tripod, with your camera attached to it. These are great for overhead shots.

If you do purchase a lighter tripod - and there's nothing wrong with that, I would recommend running to your local DIY store and grabbing a sandbag to weigh it down so as to prevent disaster. You can purchase specially made photography sandbags, but; your local DIY store is the cheaper option.

If the tripod you choose doesn't already come with one, you're going to need a tripod head. Something that will enable you to mount your camera to the tripod. Again, you generally get what you pay for with these options and I always recommend Manfrotto. There are tons of available options from ball heads, video, pan etc. Once again, think about what you need. I always recommend a three-way pan/tilt head. This allows you to control the position of the camera on every access.

Cable Release

A cable release is a cable that plugs into your camera and allows you to press the shutter and trigger the camera without touching it. This is great when you're using very low shutter speed where even the motion of you pressing the shutter will move the camera too much. You don't need this accessory, it isn't essential. You can achieve the same result with your cameras self-timer but if you have the cash or don't want to wait around for the self-timer to go off, it's an excellent alternative.

Tethering Cable

A tethering cable is used in attaching a camera to a computer. It allows you to use programs such as Lightroom Tethered Capture or Capture One. These programs make it easy to control your camera through a computer and instantly download the image for a real-time view of what you are capturing. These programs are great for things like flat lays where the camera is too high up for you to see the screen. Instead, you can see the captured image on the computer screen.

With tethering cables, you always get what you pay for. I have gone through hundreds of cheap cables; they create an annoying lag between the camera capturing the image and when you view it on a screen. They can also cause problems with saving images, image corruption or crashing the entire program.

Sync Leads (flash photography)

If you're looking into flash photography, you're going to need a way to control the lights, a way for the camera to tell the light when it's to go off. A sync lead or a wireless flash trigger does this for you. A sync lead is a cable that plugs into your camera that syncs with the lights letting them know when to trigger.

A wireless flash trigger is a device that plugs into your cameras hot shoe while another device plugs into the lights. These do the same jobs, just without the wires. This can be essential in a studio environment where tripping over wires is a real issue.

Camera Basics

One of the most important things for fledgling food photographers to grasp is their camera equipment. I'd say that THE most crucial step to improving your food photography would be to take your camera off auto mode and begin the process of mastering manual mode. Getting to grips with your camera's settings can be a daunting task, with all the buttons, dials, and menus. But, I'm here to help you master your camera to capture the very best food images.

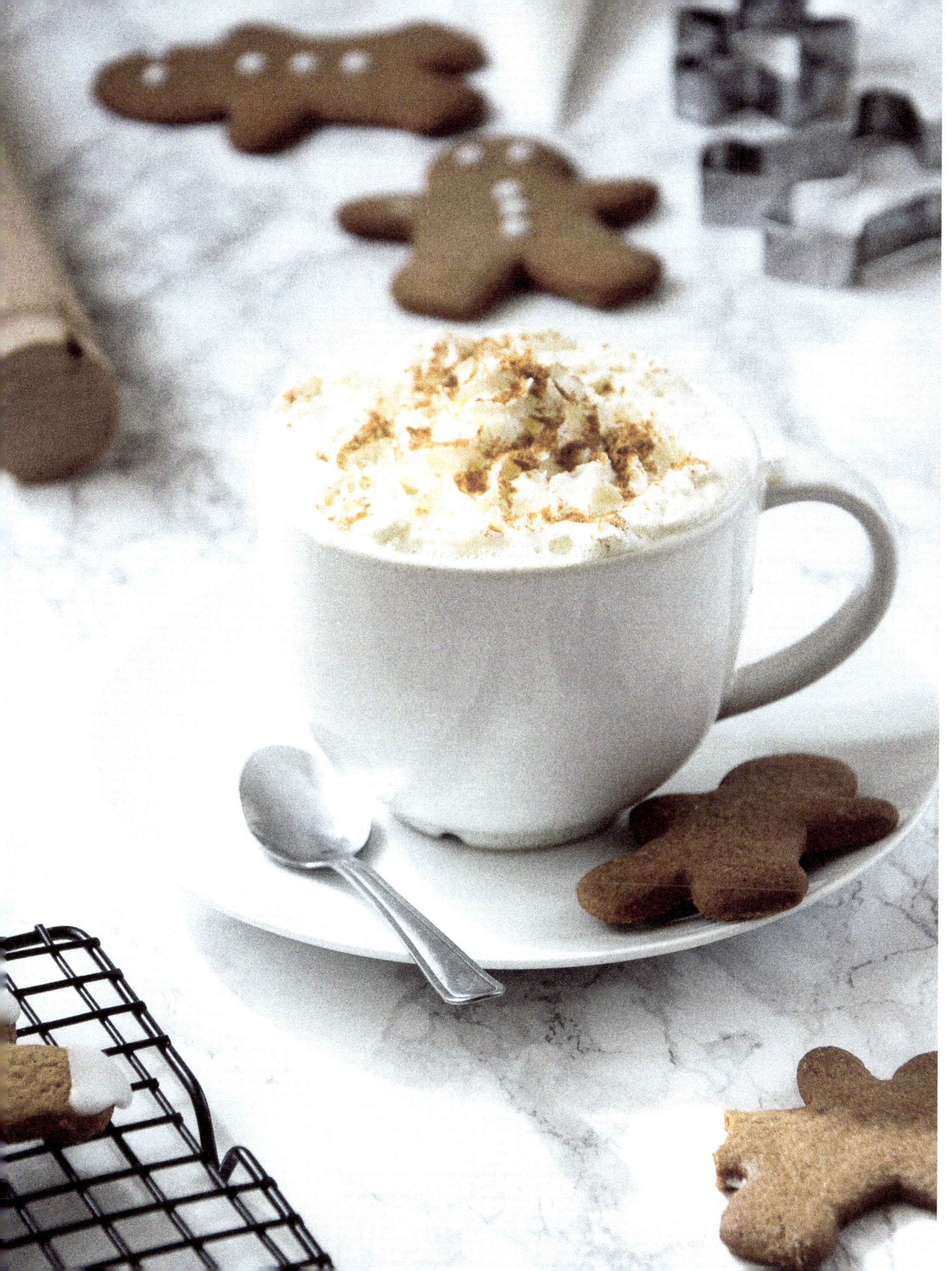

Camera basics for food photographers

The first step is switching your camera to manual mode. On most cameras, this is located on the top dial. But all cameras may likely be different. The basic modes to choose from will be Auto, marked usually with an Auto, where the camera has full control of settings. Shutter priority marked with an S, where you will set the shutter speed manually and the camera will do the rest. We will go through shutter speed later but this setting is useful when you need to freeze or blur motion and you require the camera to do the rest. The next setting will be Aperture priority, marked with an A, in which you choose the camera's aperture and the camera does the rest. This is useful if you want a large aperture to blur the background of your subject or a small aperture to get everything in the image in focus. What we're talking about today is Manual mode, where you have complete creative freedom over the camera settings. This mode is usually marked with an M.

What is exposure?

Simply put, exposure is the amount of light that reaches your camera sensor. Your exposure defines how light or dark the image will be.
There are three settings on your camera that affect your exposure, Shutter speed, Aperture, and ISO. The balance of the three will hopefully, result in a perfectly exposed image.

For every scene, there are many different combinations of shutter speed, aperture, and ISO that will result in a well-lit photograph. However, a well-exposed image doesn't necessarily equal a good image. The different setting affects the photographs differently and determines the sharpness, grain, and focus of the image.

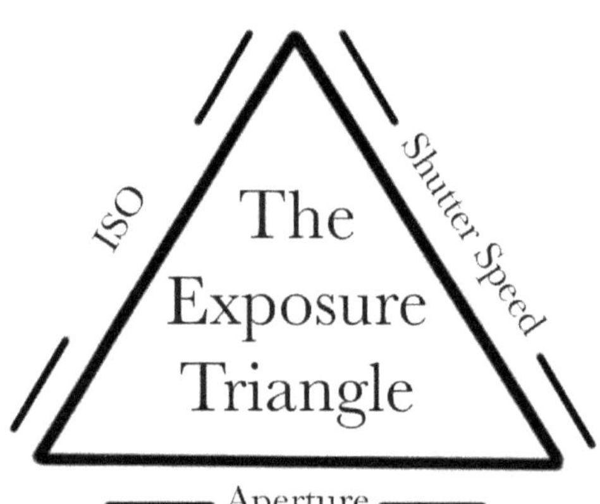

What is Aperture?

Aperture settings on a camera refers to the amount of light that the aperture ring allows to reach your sensor. Inside the lens, every camera has a ring of blades that open and close to regulate the amount of light that is let in. The size of the hole is measured in F-stops, most basic DSLR cameras and lenses will have an f-stop range of at least F4-F22. Which is generally considered the bare minimum. F-stops are expressed as fractions of 1/x. An f-stop of 2 means the aperture is half open (1/2), whereas an aperture of 11 means that the aperture is only 1/11th open. This simply means, the smaller the number, the wider the hole. When someone refers to an aperture as small or large, they refer to the hole size rather than the number. Also, if someone refers to a high or low aperture, they refer to the numerical f-stop number not the size of the hole.

When shopping for a food photography camera, it is wise to look for a camera or a lens that has the largest aperture possible. Food is often best photographed in natural light, which can sometimes be lacking and very small apertures of f2 or even lower for they very useful to let in as much light as possible.

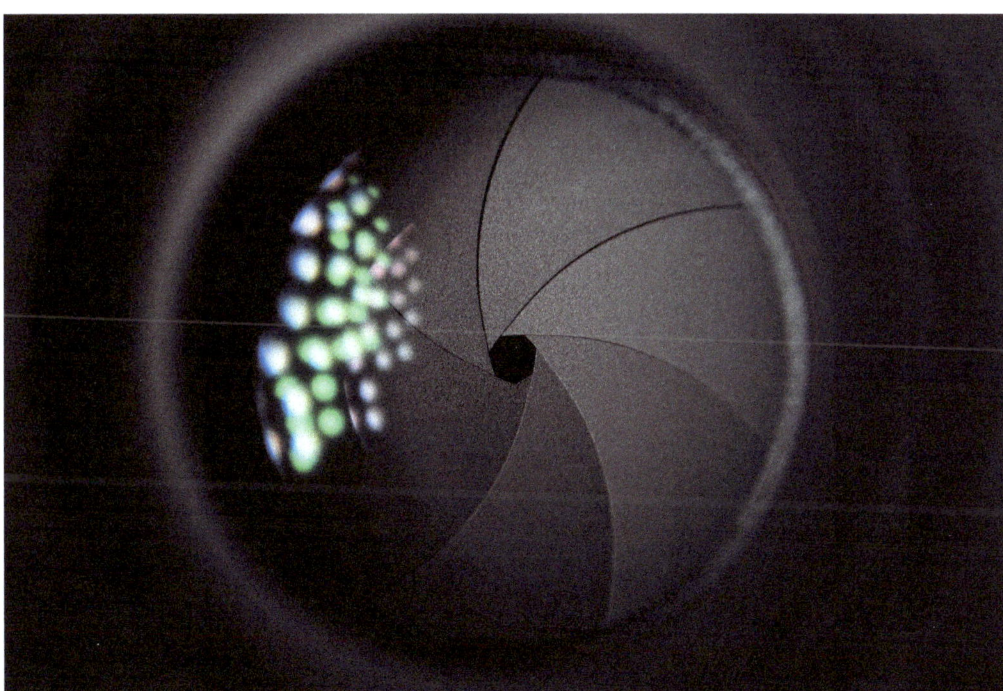

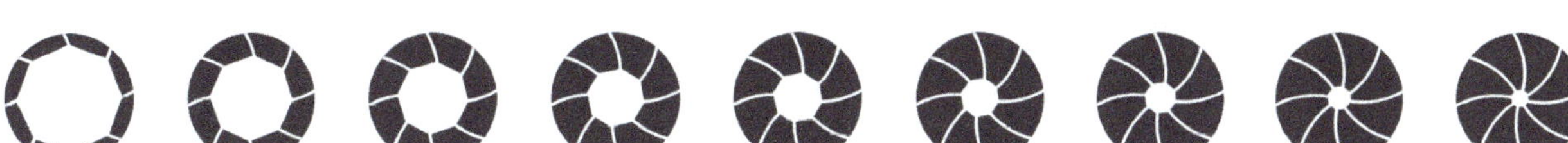

Depth of Field

In addition to controlling how much light is let into the camera, the aperture also controls the Depth of Field. Often abbreviated to DOF, Depth of Field basically refers to how much of your image is in focus. A low f-stop will result in a shallow depth of field, where only the portion of the image you have focused on is sharp and the rest is blurred. Therefore, a high f-stop will result in the image being sharp from the foreground right up to the background.

This knowledge is particularly useful in food photography and is also why I recommend buying a camera or lens with low aperture capability. A shallow depth of field blurs the background of the image making the subject pop in the frame. This is why most food photographers use a shallow depth of field in their food images.

Some lenses have very low aperture capabilities and although it is tempting to go super wide, for example, F1.8, sometimes this is just too wide and the depth of field is just too shallow. Only capturing a tiny portion of your image in focus has its advantages but you generally want most of your subject to be crisp and clear.

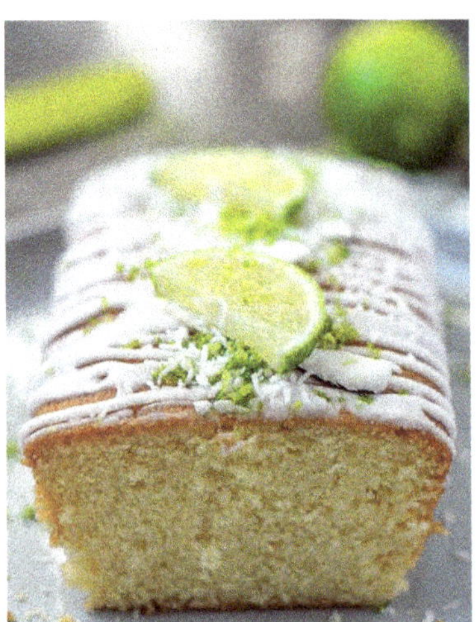

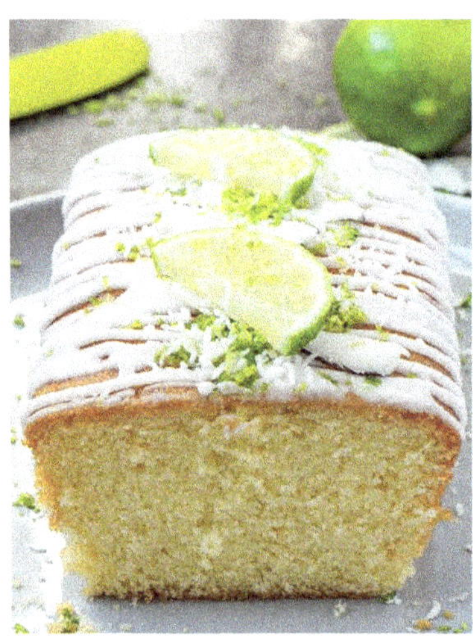

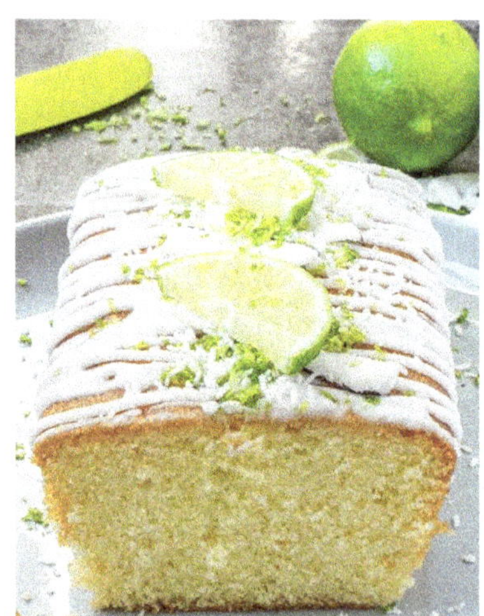

Shutter Speed

Your cameras shutter speed simply refers to the speed at which the camera's shutter opens and closes. A camera works by allowing light through a hole and onto a light-sensitive material, in modern digital cameras, this is a sensor. But the amount of time a light is allowed to reach the sensor has to be controlled and this is where the shutter comes in. The shutter opens briefly thereby allowing light to hit the sensor then closes again to complete the exposure. Shutter speed is expressed in fractions of a second, however, this will be displayed as a whole number on your camera. For example, if the shutter speed on your camera displays 100, this refers to 1/100th of a second. Camera sensors are very sensitive to light and often only need a split second of light. This means that the higher the number, the less time the shutter is open for, so less light is getting to the sensor.

When to use a fast shutter speed.

Fast shutter speeds are used to freeze motion in images. The shutter is only open for a very short amount of time and freezes the action. This is helpful when photographing something which is moving at a fast pace, like a car. In food photography, fast shutter speeds are used for pour shots. Pouring coffee into a mug or milk into a bowl and you desire to freeze the stream of liquid mid-flow. This is when you will need a fast shutter speed. To balance the exposure, you will need to adjust either the ISO or the aperture to counter the lack of light getting to the camera sensor.

Slow Shutter Speeds

There are few instances in food photography when a slow shutter speed would be useful for purely stylistic advantages. Slow shutter speeds are generally used in conjunction with a tripod in low light situations to brighten an image. Low shutter speeds should always be used with a tripod to keep the camera steady.

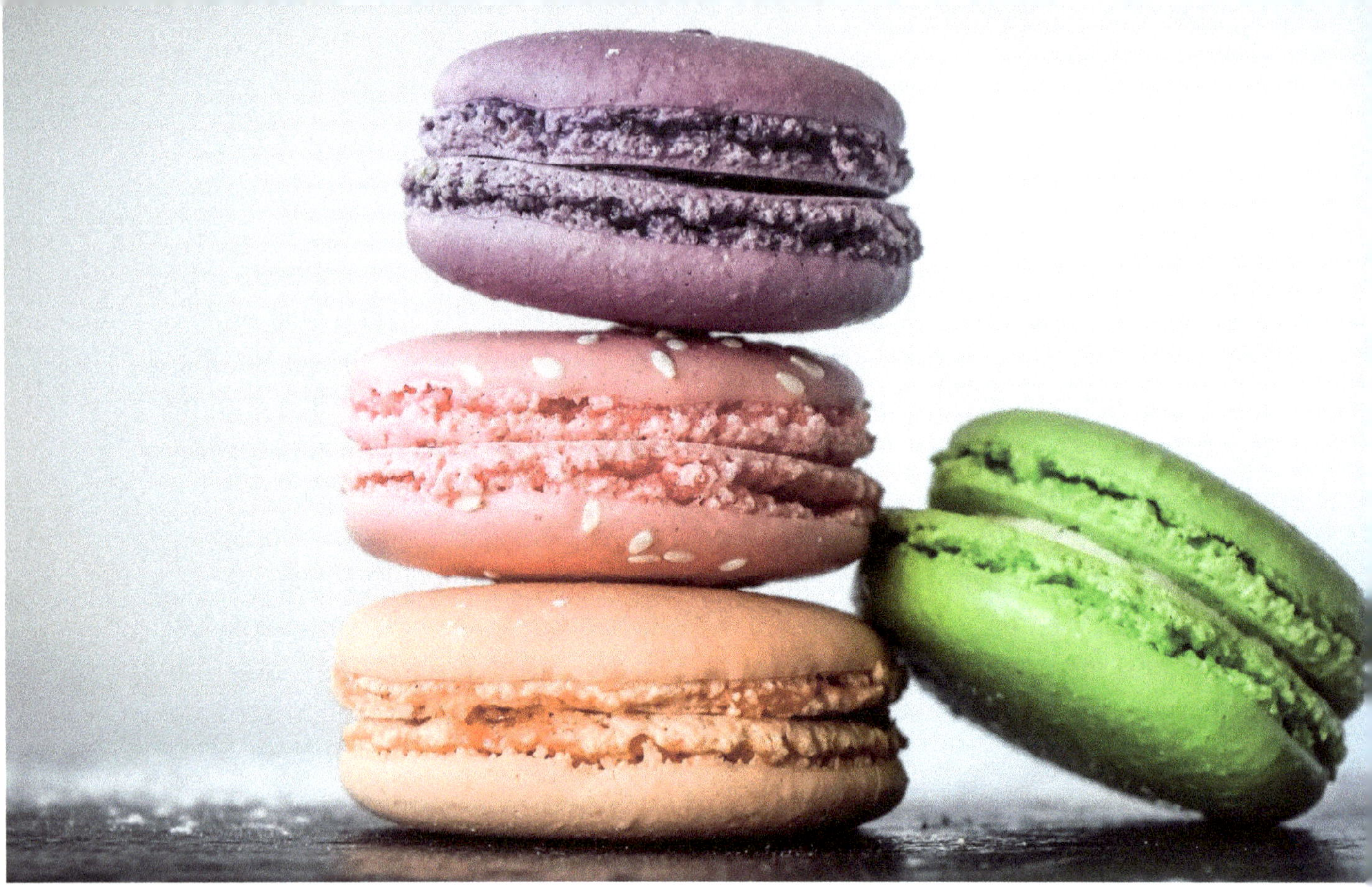

Using a tripod.

The longer you leave the shutter open, the more likely your image will be blurry. In the time that the shutter is open, something in the scene may move, or more likely, the camera will move which leaves you with motion blur. To counter this, it is generally accepted that 1/80th is the slowest shutter speed at which you can handhold a camera. If you have peculiarly shaky hands like mine, you may need a higher shutter speed to counteract your shaky hands. If you need to drop your shutter speed to anything lower than 1/80th of a second; you will need to mount your camera on a tripod to avoid shaking.

Using artificial light

Although it is widely agreed that natural light is best for food photography, sometimes it is not practical to wait around for the perfect lighting. If you decide to purchase artificial lighting for your food photography, you will need to remember that most lights that uses flash will only sync with your camera up to about 1/250th of a second. Of course, there are dedicated flashes out there that will sync much faster. But they are very expensive and specialized pieces of equipment.

ISO

In the early days of photography, the ISO referred to the film speed, or how sensitive to light the film was. A low ISO of 100 is the least sensitive to light producing the darkest images but with little noise. A high ISO of 6400 is more sensitive to light thus producing a brighter image but produces more noise in the image. As camera technology improves so does their ability to use higher ISOs with less noise. Increasing your cameras ISO is useful in low light situations when even when the aperture is wide open and your shutter speed is the lowest you can hold the camera still and it still isn't enough. Noisy images generally aren't something you need to worry about if your only posting small images on the web but if you need large high-quality images or are planning on printing this will begin to be a problem. To avoid noise, try to keep your ISO to lower than 1600 to keep noise to a minimum.

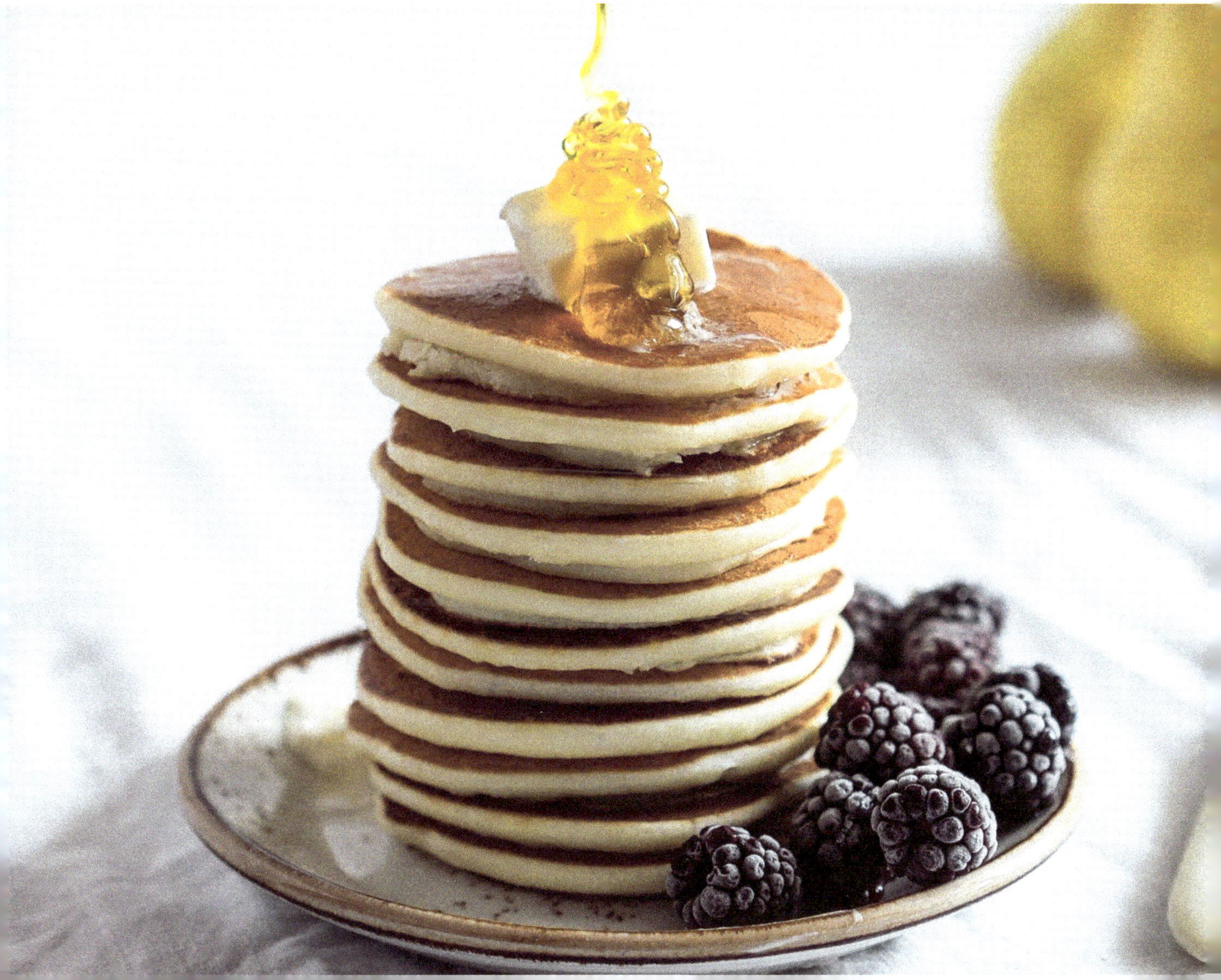

White Balance

Getting your colors right starts with your white balance. This is simple to do in camera and only takes 1 adjustment. Light color temperature is measured in Kelvins, expressed as a K. Instead of trying to memorize the exact color temperature of different situations most cameras are equipped with pre-sets to help. The most common pre-sets are cloudy, shade, bright sun, fluorescent, and tungsten. However, most cameras these days do a fantastic job in auto mode.. To set my white balance I always start by adding something white to the image, even if it isn't going to stay there, I use this as a reference. Most cameras have great auto white balance these days but if yours is struggling it's probably time to set it manually. If you are shooting in natural light with a light diffuser you will probably need either the cloud or the shade setting. Choose whichever setting gets the white object in the scene as close to white as possible and take a photo with the white object in for reference later.

If you have Lightroom or similar editing software you can tweak the white balance more using the built-in white balance tool. Choose the white area of the image then simply apply the settings to all of the images you need to fix the white balance on. You can also do this manually by adding blue or orange to the image depending on which it needs. If the image is too warm, add blue and if it's too blue add orange.

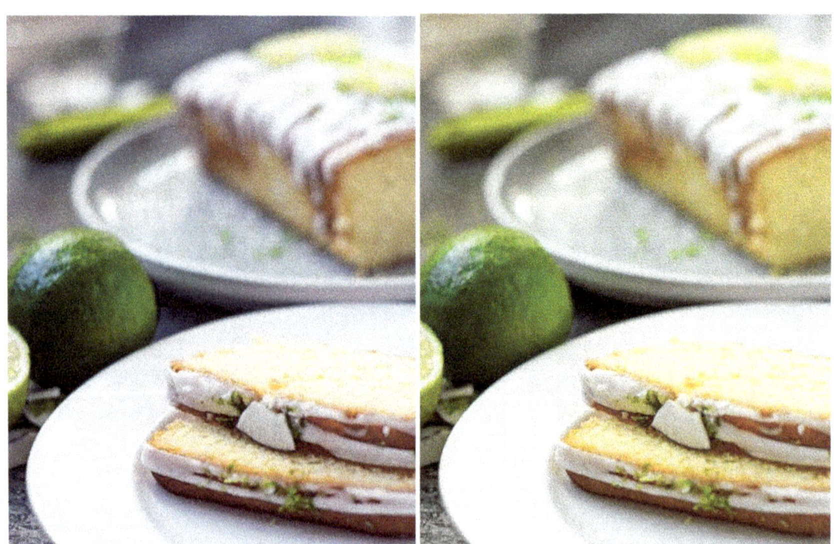

Two examples of off white balance.
Left: too blue
Right: too yellow

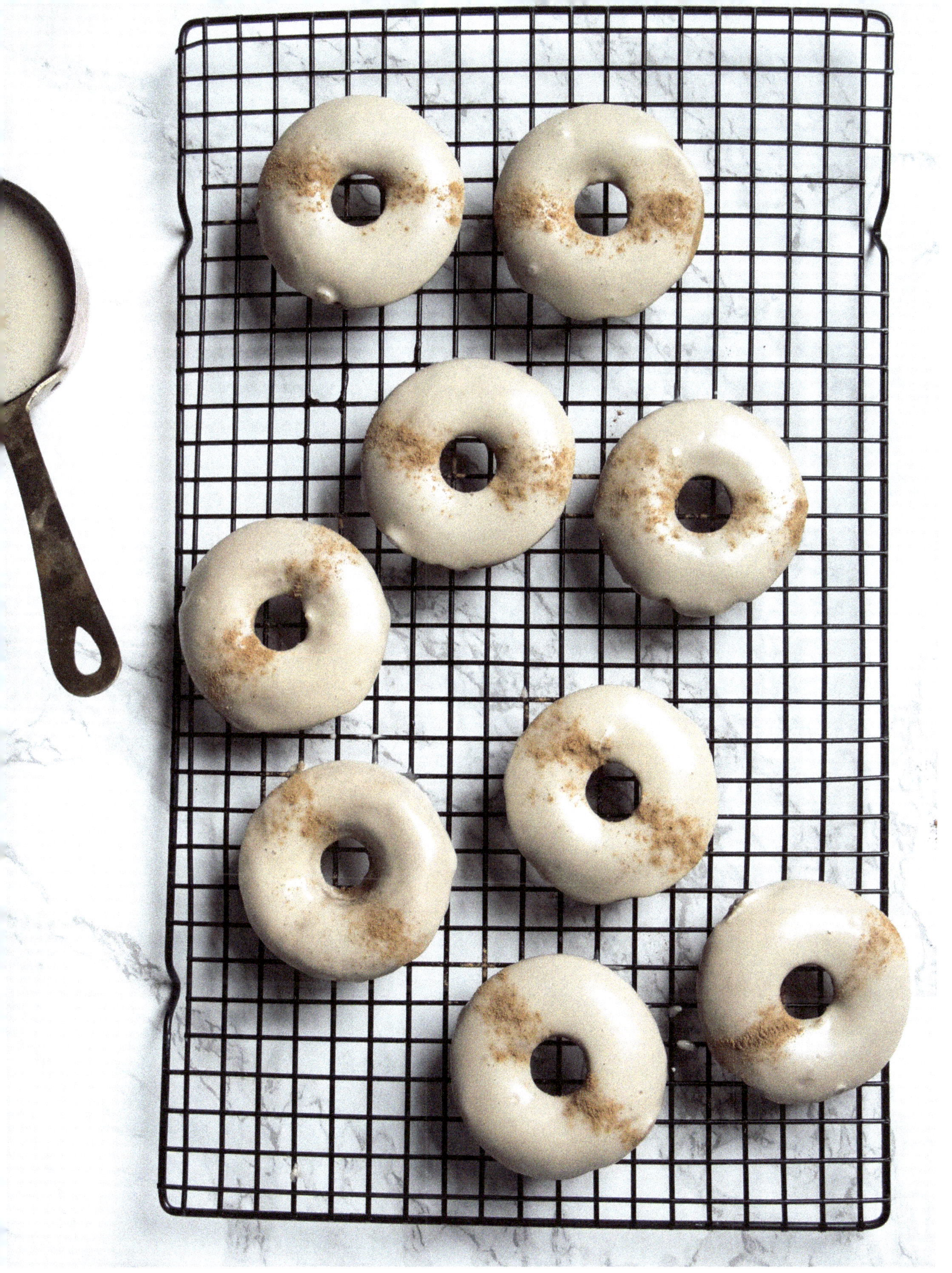

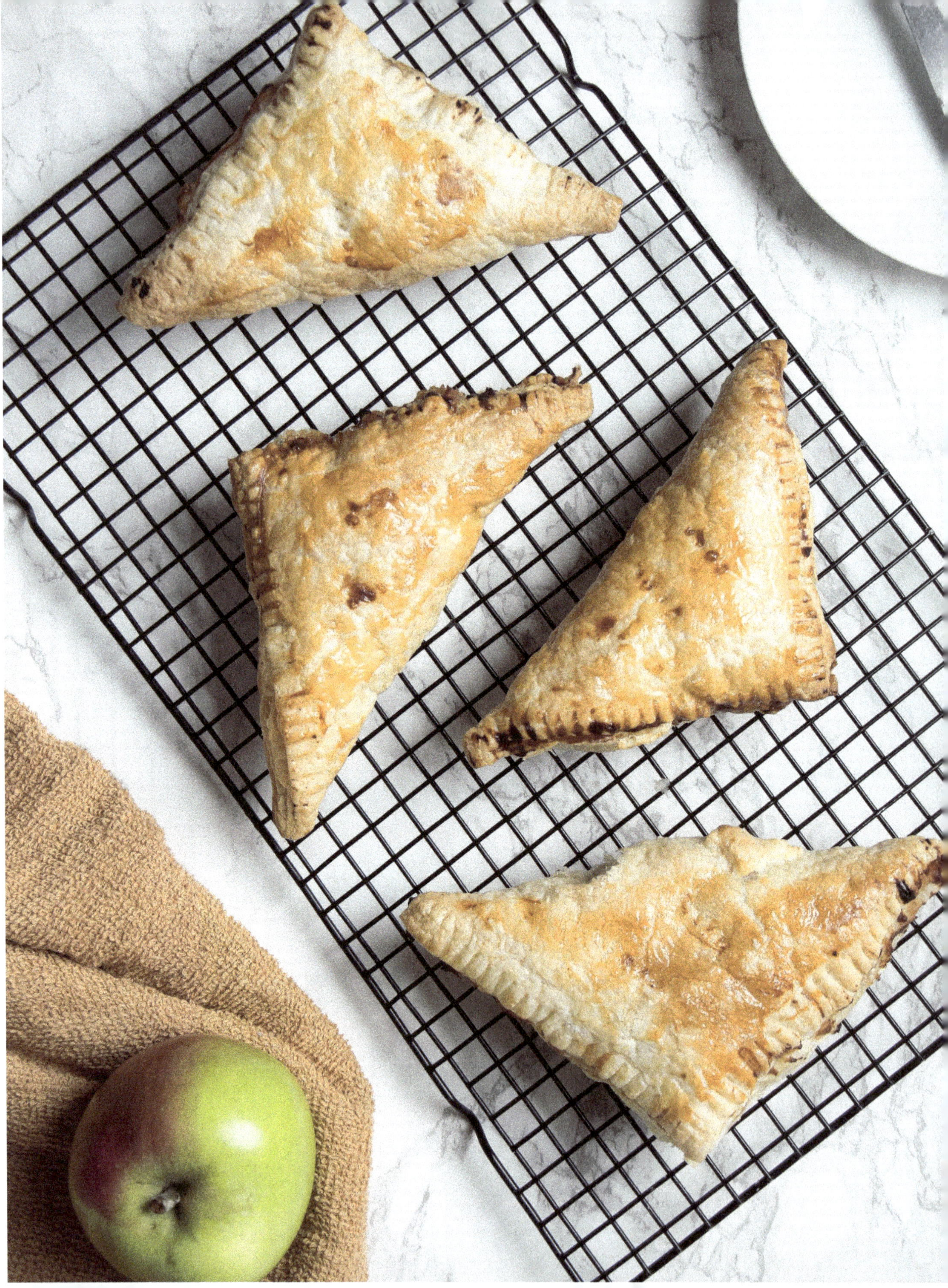

Raw vs JPEG

When looking through the menu of your digital camera, you will see that you have the choice of two options for your images. You can shoot RAW images or JPEG. Some older cameras may only let you shoot JPEGS but these days, almost every DSLR or mirrorless camera will have RAW capabilities.

The main difference between RAW and JPEG is post-processing capabilities. You have a lot more options and freedom when editing your images with a RAW format. Raw images allow for editing the image non-destructively, which means that any changes you make can be erased. And you can start over without any negative alteration to the image. JPEGS, on the other hand, have all of their settings "baked in" which means that they can't be changed. You can tweak the image a little, but too much editing will negatively alter and affect the image.

When shooting RAW, the ability to edit the image without negatively affecting it afterward is essential to most photographers. Using editing software like Photoshop and Lightroom, you can accurately fix white balance and ensure that your colors are always true to life. Properly colored and balanced images are essential in food photography.

RAW	vs	JPEG
<u>Advantage of RAW</u>		<u>Advantage of JPEG</u>
wide dynamic range		small file size
ability to make white balance and exposure changes in post		little editing needed
<u>Disdvantage of RAW</u>		<u>Disdvantage of JPEG</u>
large file size		editing causes loss of detail and image quality
needs specialist editing software and knowledge		exposure and white balance must be acurate in camera

Working with Light

The best thing about food photography is that as far as lighting is concerned, less is more. Natural light is hailed as the holy grail of food photography lighting, and all you need to achieve this is a window. Now, if you can't always sync your shooting schedule with the sun, this is when you need to start to look at an artificial lighting option. But again, the simplest solution is often the best, one light with a few reflectors often produces the best results.

Lighting is without a doubt the most important element of producing amazing food images, and this is where you should invest your time and money if you're just starting out. Take some time to study the types of light discussed below and see which solutions fit your situation.

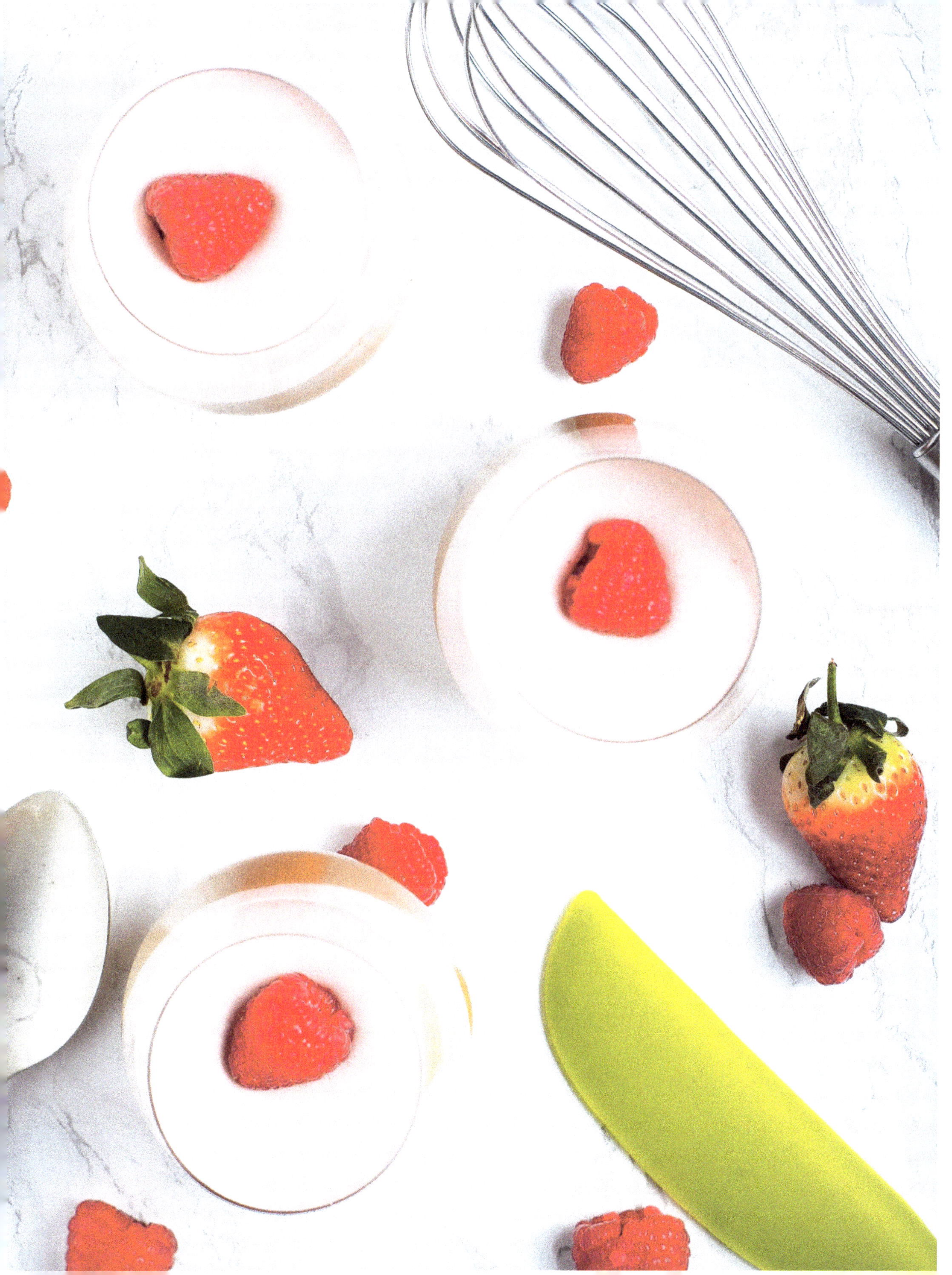

Types of light

Natural Light

Natural light is the holy grail of light when photographing food. It's soft, bright, free and easy to use. All you need is a window. If you photograph your food at home, it's worth taking some time to move your setups to different parts of the house to see which window will produce the best result. Often, kitchen windows are not the biggest or brightest in the house.

I love working with natural light because it's soft, so it gives you beautiful and delicate shadows. It's also super easy to use, there's no setting up of lights, just throw your table by the window, add some reflectors and shoot...it's that simple. When I shoot at home, I actually use my bedroom window, it's huge, faces the sun and is very low to the floor, and I don't even need to set up a table.

One thing you need to remember with natural light is that brighter is not necessarily better. The best light for food photography is indirect, diffused light. We'll talk more about light diffusers later but bright sunny days, where direct sunlight is streaming through the window is not what you want. Bright, overcast days are better or you're going to have to use a diffuser.

Artificial Light

Although natural light is best, it is very constricting. Artificial light gives you the freedom to shoot anytime and anywhere. With natural light, you are restricted to shooting right next to a window, but with artificial light, you can take your set up anywhere. Also, with natural light, you have to shoot during the day and you have to sit around waiting for the right light. With artificial light, you have the freedom to shoot whenever you want and you always have the right light.

Artificial light does take some practice to get used to. With so much freedom, it's often confusing where to start. It's important to remember that with artificial light we are trying to replicate natural light. So, we want our light source to be large and soft. We'll talk more about how to achieve this later.

Artificial light for food comes in two forms, flash or continuous light. Both have their pros and cons and if artificial light is something that you want to invest in, it's going to come down to what is right for you.

Flash

Flash or strobe lights come in two options, small flash heads or studio lights. Small flash heads are designed to be attached to your camera and they are what you see wedding or event photographers use to create a large burst of light. They are an inexpensive alternative to a studio strobe light, as they can be used off camera by connecting through a sync lead. There are a small number of light modifiers available for flash heads but nowhere near the range available for studio strobes. The advantage to flash heads is that they are small, portable, and inexpensive. They are a great way to learn about artificial light or to test if it's right for you.

Studio strobe lights come in all shapes, sizes and most importantly wattages. They are the preferred choice by most food photographers because of the huge number of light modifiers available. They take up quite a bit of space and are a much more expensive option when compared to the flash head.

Continuous Light

In days gone by, continuous lighting was an absolute no go area for food photographers. Before LED lights were commercially available, the only continuous lighting available was halogen bulbs. If you've never used a halogen bulb before, let me explain that they get HOT, CRAZY HOT. So hot your ice-cream would melt in a matter of minutes.

With recent technological advances, LED light panels have become more and more accessible and affordable to an average photographer. Giving you a heat-free continuous lighting solution. These LED light panels are great because the light they produce is the exact color temperature of daylight. They are small, compact and LEDs never break so you'll never have to keep spare bulbs handy. Currently, they are still on the expensive side for a quality unit, but cheaper brands are available for a good price if you just want to try them out.

Continuous light is very much what you see is what you get. Meaning, what your eyes see, is what the camera is going to see also. Whereas with flash, the modelling bulb is quite different from what the flash produces. This means that continuous lighting solutions are excellent for beginners just learning how to light a scene to photograph excellent images of food.

Sync Speed

When using strobe lights or any kind of flash lighting, you need to keep your shutter speed in mind. Most strobe lights will only sync with your camera up to around 1/250th of a second. Any shutter speed faster than this can result in a black image. It is possible to purchase lighting that will sync much quicker than this, however, these are highly specialized pieces of equipment and are priced accordingly.

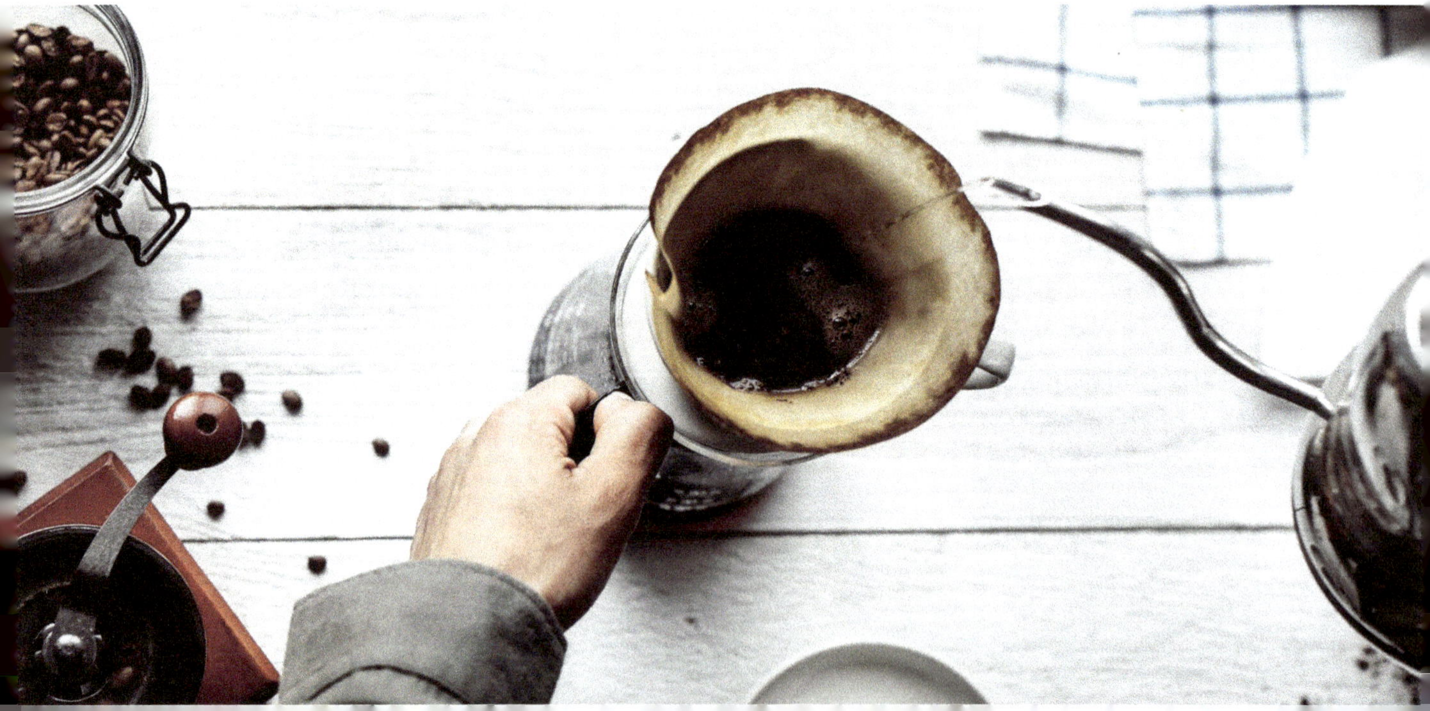

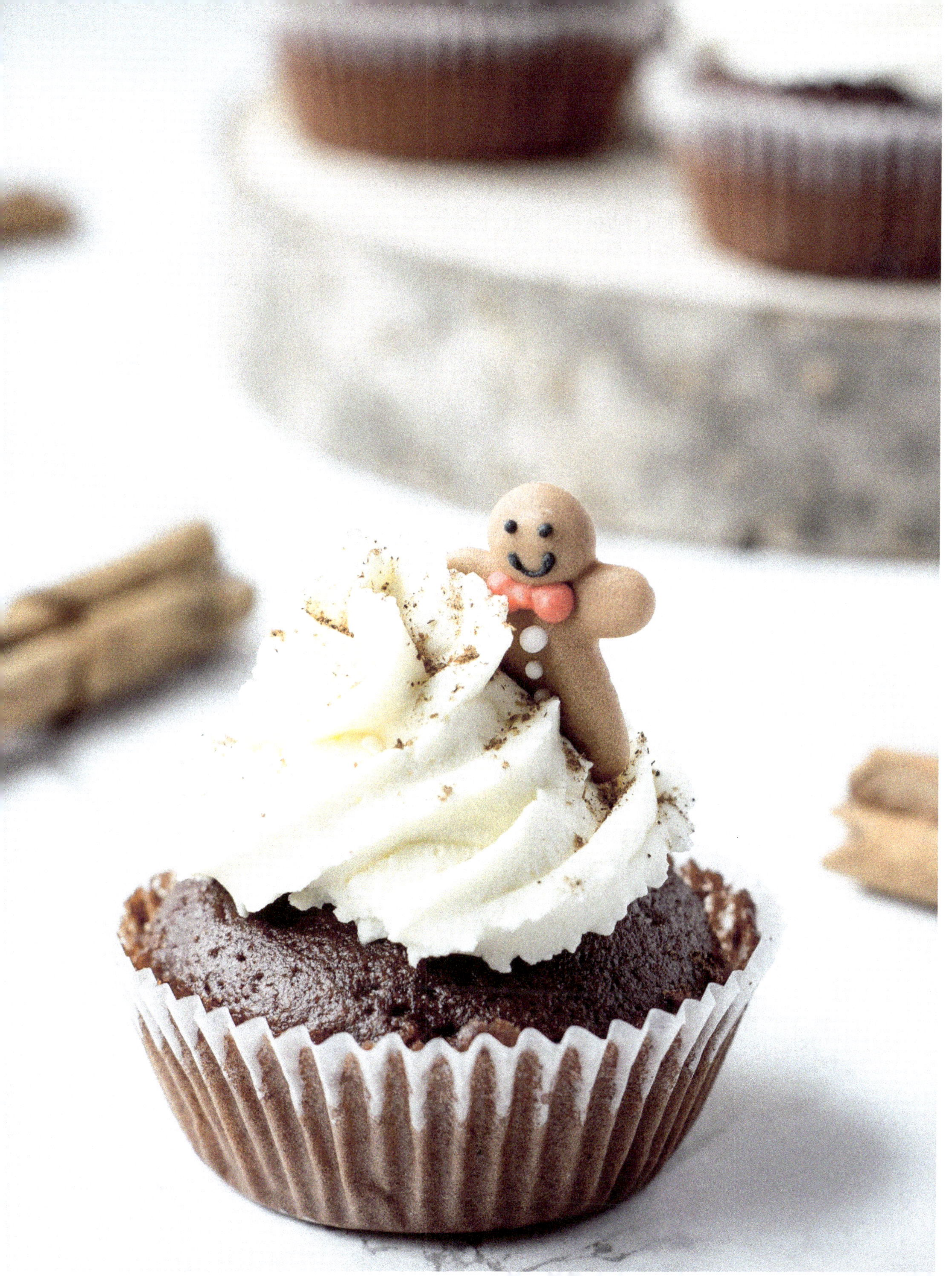

Modifying Light

No matter what type of light you use for your food photography, you're going to need some way to control that light. This is where light modifiers come in. The types of modifiers mostly used with food are reflectors, diffusers, softboxes, and umbrellas. Each one has its pros and cons and it's really up to you as to which one will suit your style.

Reflectors

Reflectors are my number one desert island light modifier. They can be used with any light source and are fairly inexpensive. As the name suggests, reflectors are anything that reflects light. Usually a whiteboard or a piece of stretched white fabric. But you can also buy silver or gold reflectors to add color to your images. No matter what you are photographing, you're probably going to need some kind of reflector.

Reflectors are used to bounce light into shadowed or darker areas to brighten them. They need to be positioned so that the light hits them and is bounced back onto the subject. A great way to practice is with a mirror. A mirror is the most extreme form of a reflector and will achieve the most dramatic result, they are, however, an excellent way to see where the light will hit. If you are learning how to use a reflector, I highly recommend grabbing a mirror to see where different positions will affect the lighting.

The best reflectors don't have to be expensive or overly complicated. My favorite reflectors are white foam board purchased from art supply stores. They're mostly a couple of dollars each, and can be bent and cut to whatever shape you want. I've been to professional studios, working for big clients that almost exclusively use foam board for reflectors.

Diffusers

Unlike reflectors, diffusers sit between your light source and subject. They come in many shapes and size and are used with both natural and artificial light. All diffusers do the same job, they all soften the light. This is essential to remove any harsh shadows which are often unpleasant with food.

It's important to remember that the bigger your light source and the closer it is to your subject, the softer your light will be. Diffusers make your light source larger because they take the concentrated light from a bulb or the sun and they spread it over a larger surface.

Diffusion Panel

A diffusion panel is a large piece of fabric that is placed between your light source and your subject. Purchased diffusion panels are often a piece of white fabric stretched around a wire frame. These come in a variety of sizes and shapes and you can find them to suit every budget. An advantage to these is that they can often be folded down for easy storage.

If you don't want to purchase a diffusion panel and are using natural light, you can always make your own. All you need is white fabric and space to hang it in front of a window or a lightweight frame to stretch it around. In the past, I've made diffusion panels from plumbing pipes, fitting them together to make a frame and then sewing elastic around a piece of white fabric cut to size so that it can be stretched over the frame. If you get creative, there are lots of DIY options available.

I don't recommend making your own diffusers when using flash because the bulbs can get hot and be a fire risk. Always use professional products when working with flash heads as purposely made diffusers will be made from fire retardant material that is designed for the job. That being said, it's never a good idea to lean anything right up against your flashbulb. This is why softboxes and umbrellas exist. LED light panels are different because they don't conduct heat.

Softboxes

If you decide that you want to use artificial lighting, softboxes are an essential tool for modifying your light. They are designed to diffuse and spread your light to make it soft and even. They are essential if you want to minimize harsh shadows in your images.

The disadvantage of softboxes is that they are large and bulky. They take up a lot of space. I have softboxes that are made to fold down and pack away but I have to say that since I put them up, I have never dismantled them, it's far too much effort.

Umbrellas

A good alternative to a softbox is an umbrella. There are two different ways to use an umbrella, they can be used to diffuse the light, where the light source is shone through the umbrella onto the subject. This method produces results similar to that of a softbox.

Alternatively, the umbrella can be used as a reflector. By swapping out the white umbrella for a silver or gold version, the light can be turned away from the subject and shone into the reflective umbrella where it will bounce back at the subject.

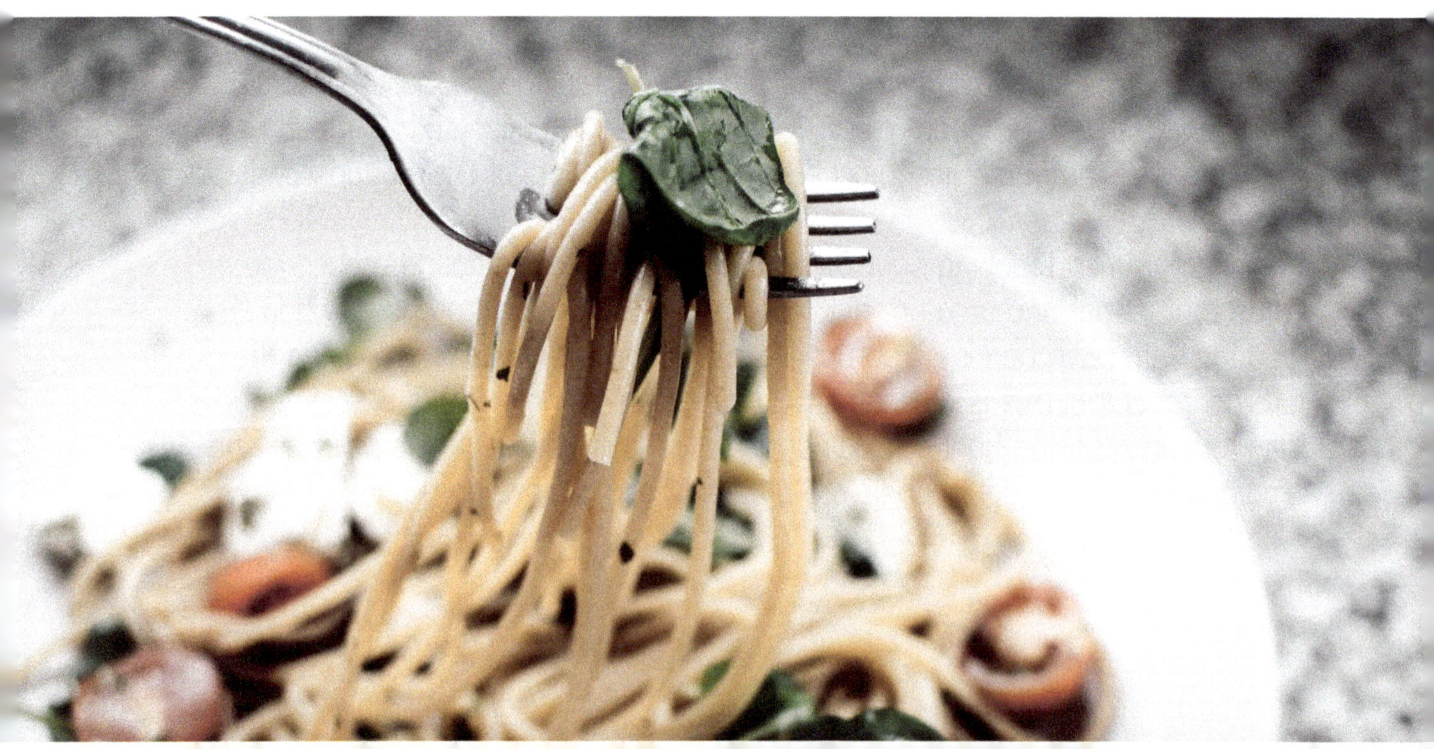

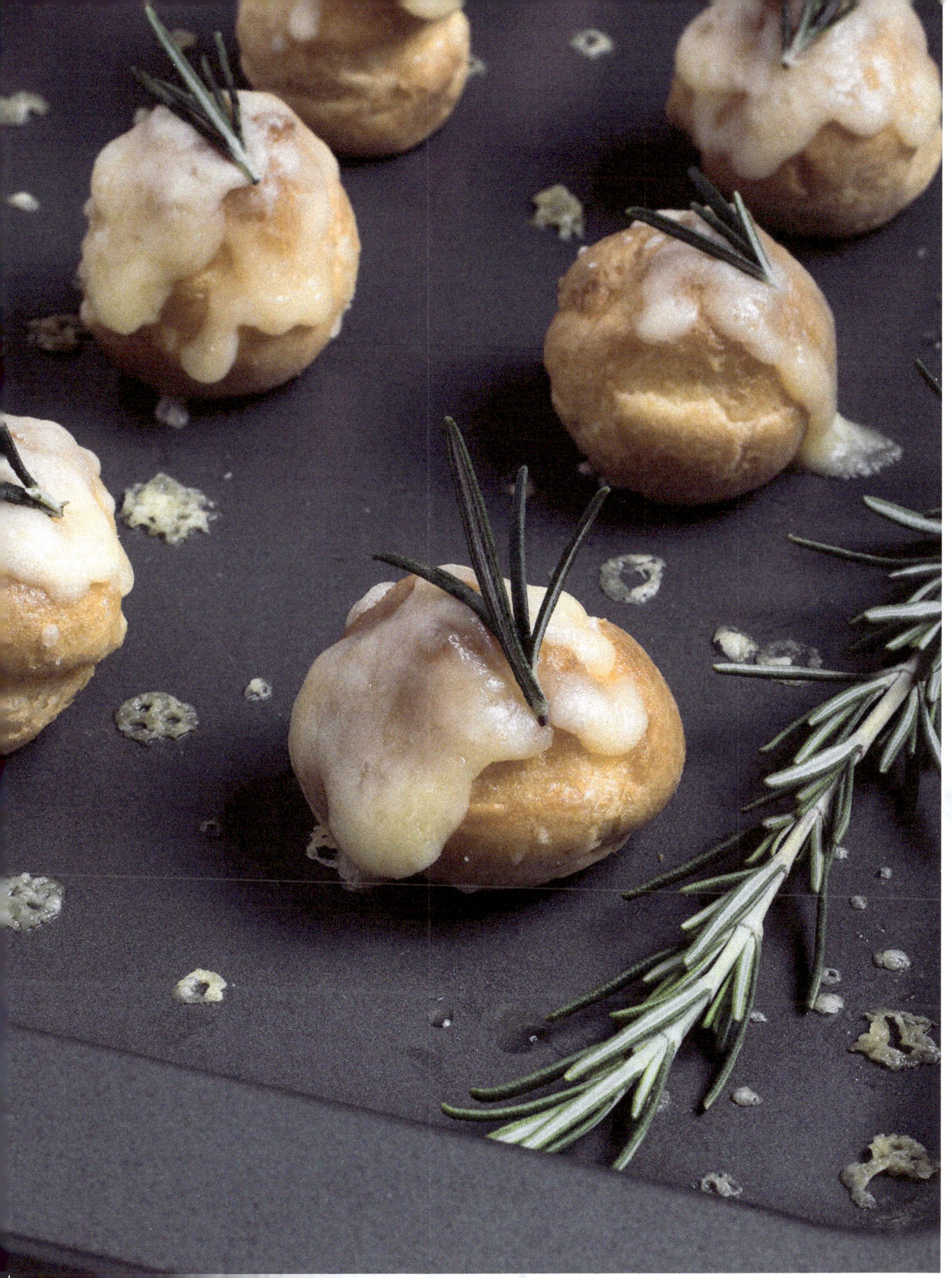

Quality of Light

All light is not made equal, there is such a thing as bad light. The light that you see from the sun on a cloudy day is quite different from what you see on a cloudless day at sunset. The light from your homes overhead bulbs is also quite different from the light produced from a LED panel.

The type of light you use will have an effect on the color, intensity, and mood of the overall lighting.

It is probably true to say that not all light is bad, rather, not all light is good for all types of photography. With the exception of your average household lightbulb for overhead lights, they're terrible for any type of photography. Portrait photographers' favor the light produced just before sunset and just after sunrise, lovingly named the "golden hour". Food photographers favor a bight yet still overcast day where the clouds provide a natural diffusion.

Different types of light create different moods with their varied colors and intensities. Working with light is about deciding on what feel of an image you are going for and choosing the right light to create that feel.

Color

The color of light that you use with food photography is essential. Color temperature with light is measured in Kelvins expressed as a K. Daylight, which is considered the best for food photography sits at around 6500K.

As a comparison, a candle flame, which is very warm, is around 1900K. A tungsten light bulb is around 2800K and the light from a shady area is around 7500K.

With Kelvin, the lower the number, the warmer or more orange the light. Subsequently, the higher the number, the colder or colored blue the light would be.

Shooting with a light source that is too far away from daylights 6500K will create a color cast in your images. With food photography, a color cast will look strange and make your food unappetizing. Using the most flattering light and correct color balance will ensure your images look their best.

In order to get the perfect white balance for your images, it is always best not to mix your light sources. If you are using natural light from a window, you do not want to contaminate that light with light from any other bulbs in your house. Remember to turn off all other light sources. This goes for artificial light too.

Intensity

When choosing your lighting, it is important to consider the intensity of the light. If you are using natural light, this is a simpler process. If you are working on an overcast day, this will likely not be a problem. But on a bright sunny day, if the sunlight is coming directly through the window, it will create harsh shadows on your scene. To reduce this, you will need some kind of diffuser between the window and your subject.

It is more important to consider intensity when using artificial light. If you purchase a very powerful strobe light, you may find that even on its lowest setting, it is too bright. This is problematic if you are using a low aperture to blur out your background. Strobe lights will only sync up to around 1/250th of a second. Once you hit that, your only option is to make your aperture smaller, which will ruin your blurred background.

In this instance, you have two options, you can add a diffuser, such as a softbox. Sometimes this alone will not be enough and you will need an additional diffusion panel between your light and subject to further lessen the light. Another option is to increase the distance between the light and the subject. However, this comes with its own consequences.

Distance

The amount of space between your light source and your subject plays a huge part in determining the softness or harshness of the light. The bigger your light source and the closer it is to your subject, the softer the light and subsequently the shadows will be.

Think of it like this, if you shine a torch on something and have it really close, the shadow is small. The further away you move that torch, the larger the shadow becomes. Couple this with a large soft light source and it's quite possible to eliminate shadows altogether.

If you want soft shadows in your images, you will need to have your light source diffused, large and as close to the subject as possible.

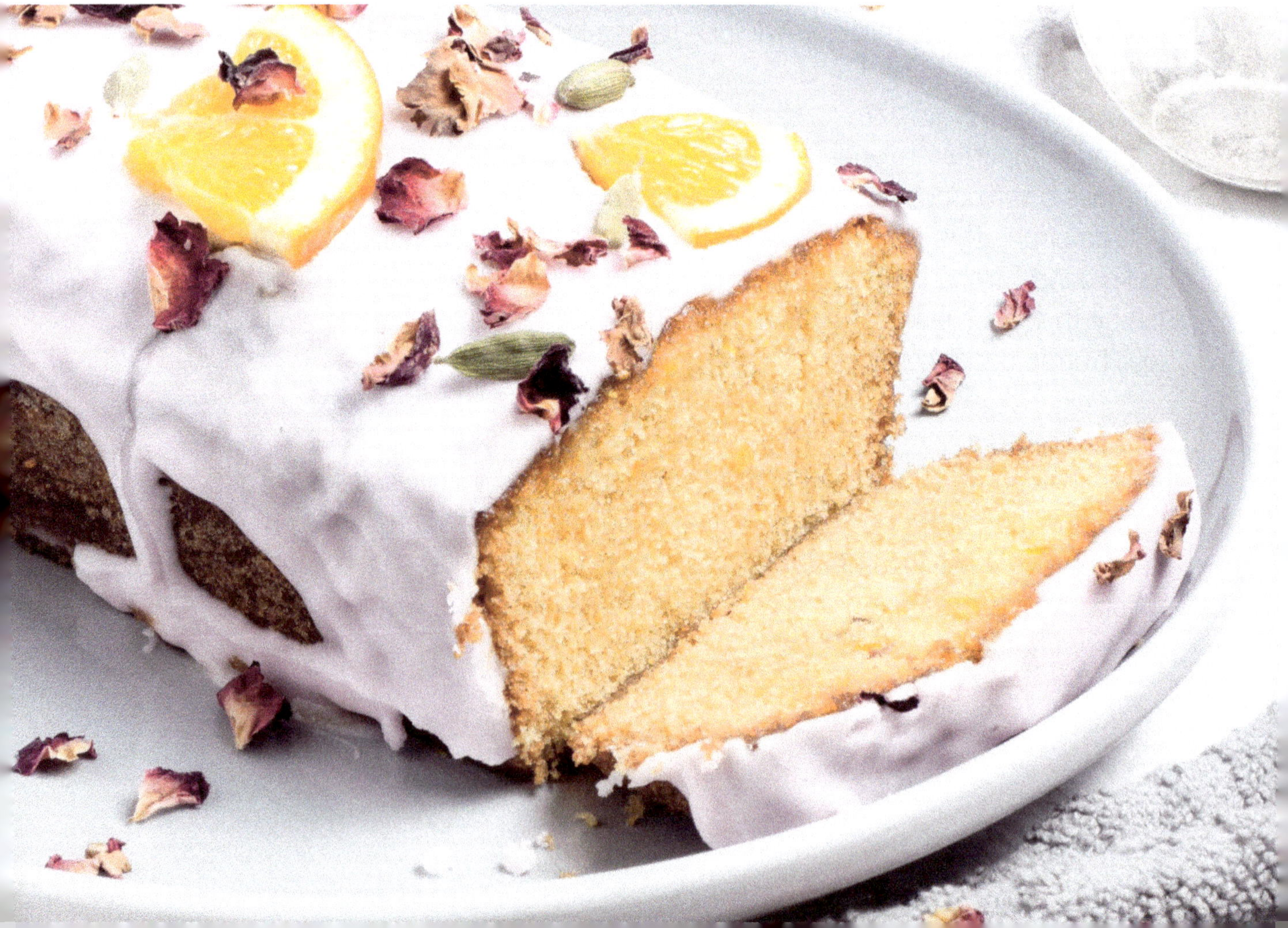

Direction of light

One last thing to consider when lighting your image is the direction of the light. The ultimate goal when lighting a scene is to make the subject as visually pleasing as possible and the direction of the light plays a big part in this. Different lighting directions will highlight different qualities of the subject and bring out different sections and textures. We're going to discuss three basic lighting directions and their effect on a subject.

Backlight

It is widely accepted that backlighting is the best lighting for food images because it adds texture and depth to an image. Backlighting is a simple set up, the light is placed directly behind your subject. Reflectors are used to bounce the light on the sides of the subject which then spills round to the front.

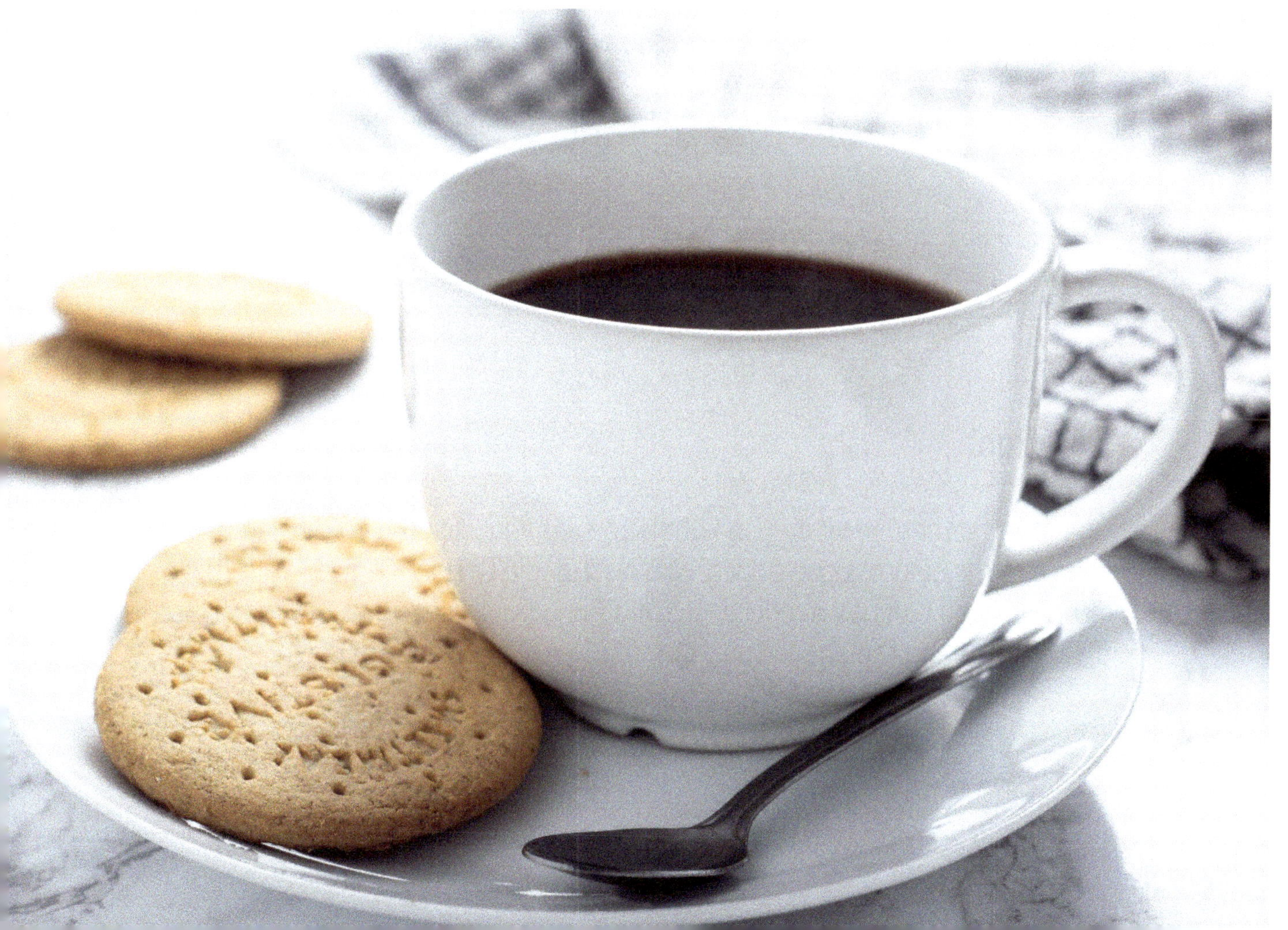

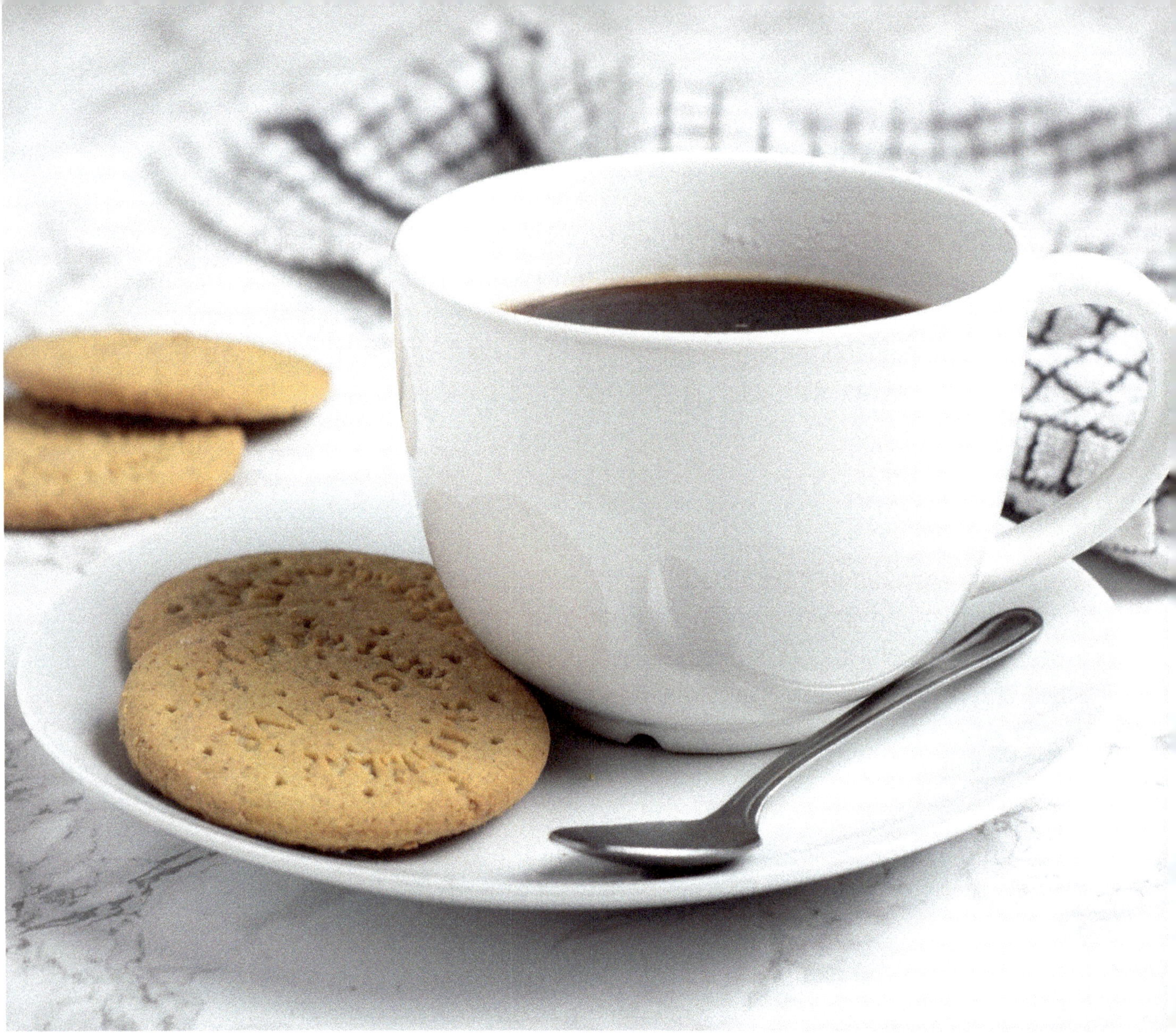

Sidelight

One of my favorite ways to use light is to side light. Created by placing your light source to the side of your subject at a right angle to your camera. With this technique, you can use a reflector to fill in any harsh shadows created or use the option of leaving the shadows to give the image contrast and depth.

Frontlight

I have to admit that I almost never use front light when capturing food. But if you do choose this lighting set up, you must ensure that the light is very soft and pleasing. Front lighting often results in a much darker background because you are taking your meter reading from the food, which will be the brightest part of the image. This can sometimes be what you are going for and I have seen a lot of photographers use this technique to create beautifully dark, moody food photography.

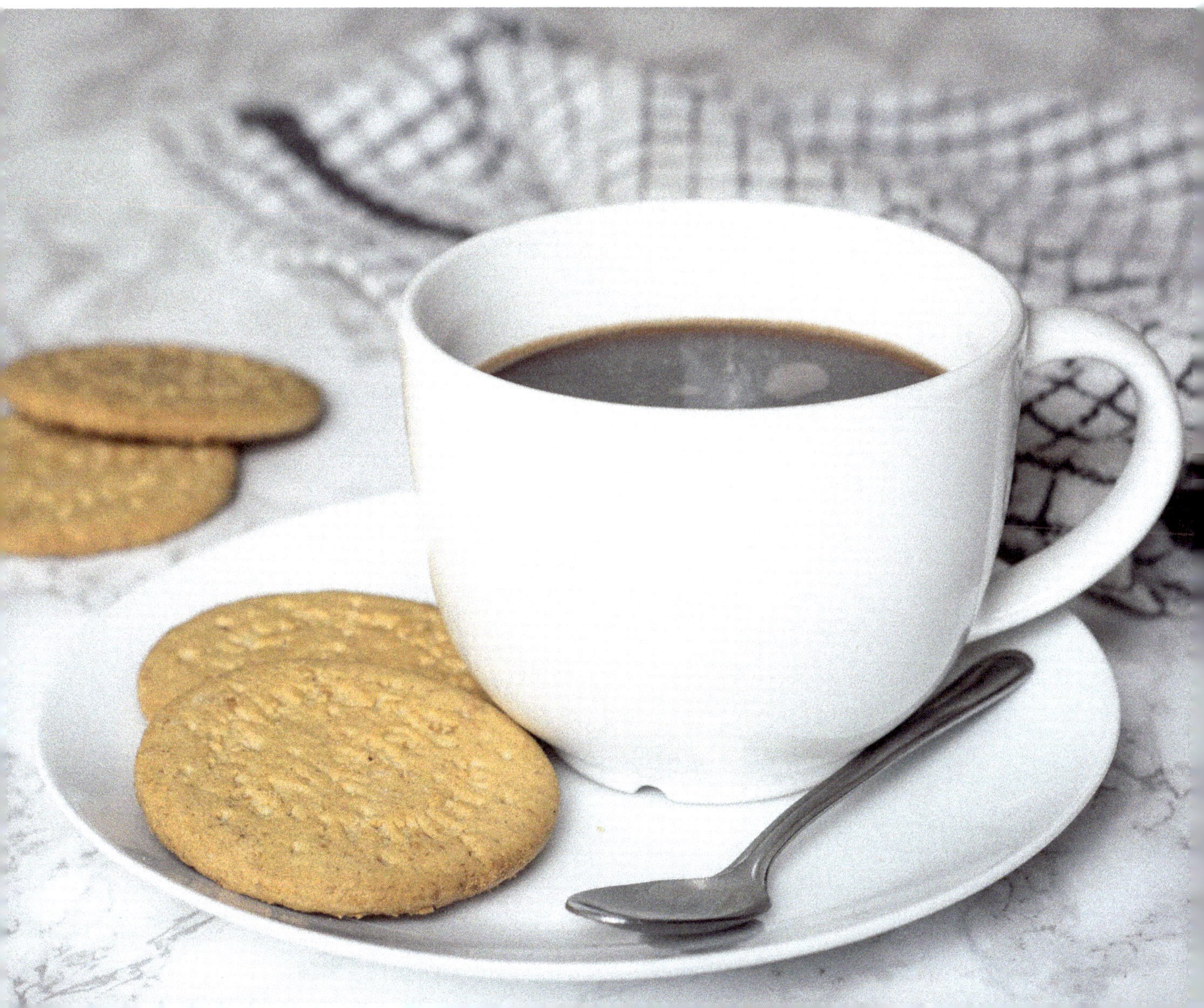

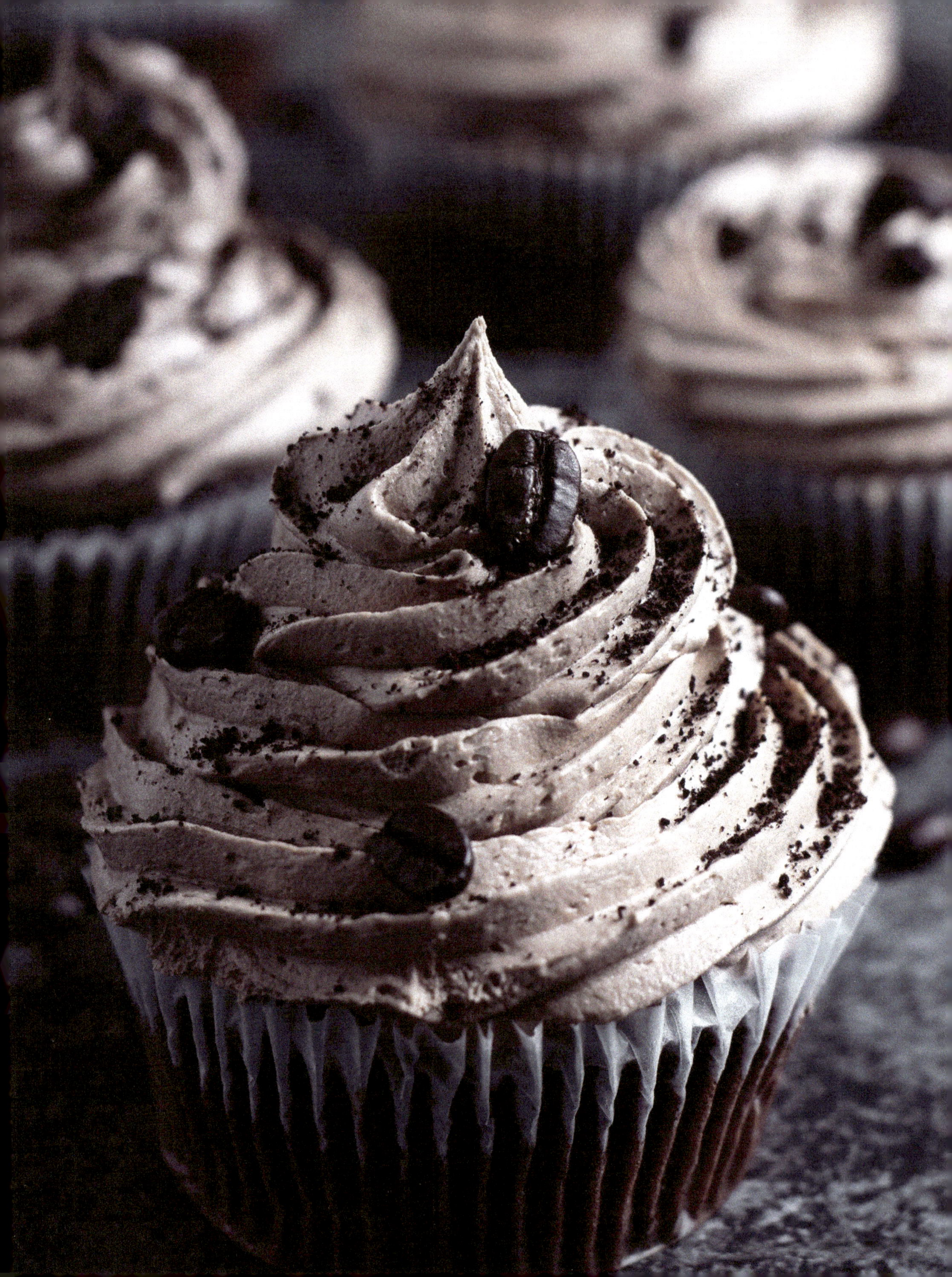

UNDERSTANDING COMPOSITION

No matter what you capture, framing your images properly is very important. With food photography in particular; composition can make or break an image. Being too close or too far from your subject or shooting from an inappropriate angle are all things that can have a detrimental effect on your final image. Composition in photography is simply the arrangement of things in front of the camera and when you look at a well-composed image, you know instantly what the main subject is. A well-composed image is pleasing to view and looks balanced.

Luckily for us, taking amazing images has never been easier, camera phones these days have the potential to rival big DSLR cameras and good quality lighting can be bought cheaply and is readily available. Just think of all of the amazing Instagram accounts out there that have all been shot on smartphones. With a little bit of know-how from me and a little effort on your part, we can up your food photography game and have you smashing out Insta worthy food photos in no time.

The Rule of Thirds

The most widely used composition tool is the rule of thirds. It's widely used because it's built into most digital cameras. When taking a photograph with a digital camera, when is the last time you noticed the grid on the screen? This three by three grid makes up the rule of thirds and it says that your main subject should sit either along one of the lines or on an intersection. This works because our eyes are naturally drawn to these points. The rule of thirds has been used for decades in photography and centuries in other mediums so we are already predisposed to think that images which stick to these rules are well composed.

It's often quite simple to choose your main subject to place in the grid, it will most often be the subject of your recipe. However, sometimes you want to just highlight a certain aspect of the dish and the rule of thirds comes into play here too. Let's look at the example below. By getting in close and offsetting the part of the image we want to highlight, the viewer's eye is drawn to it. But getting in close isn't always the best, the angle you shoot at is an equally important composition tool and is something to consider when making your images.

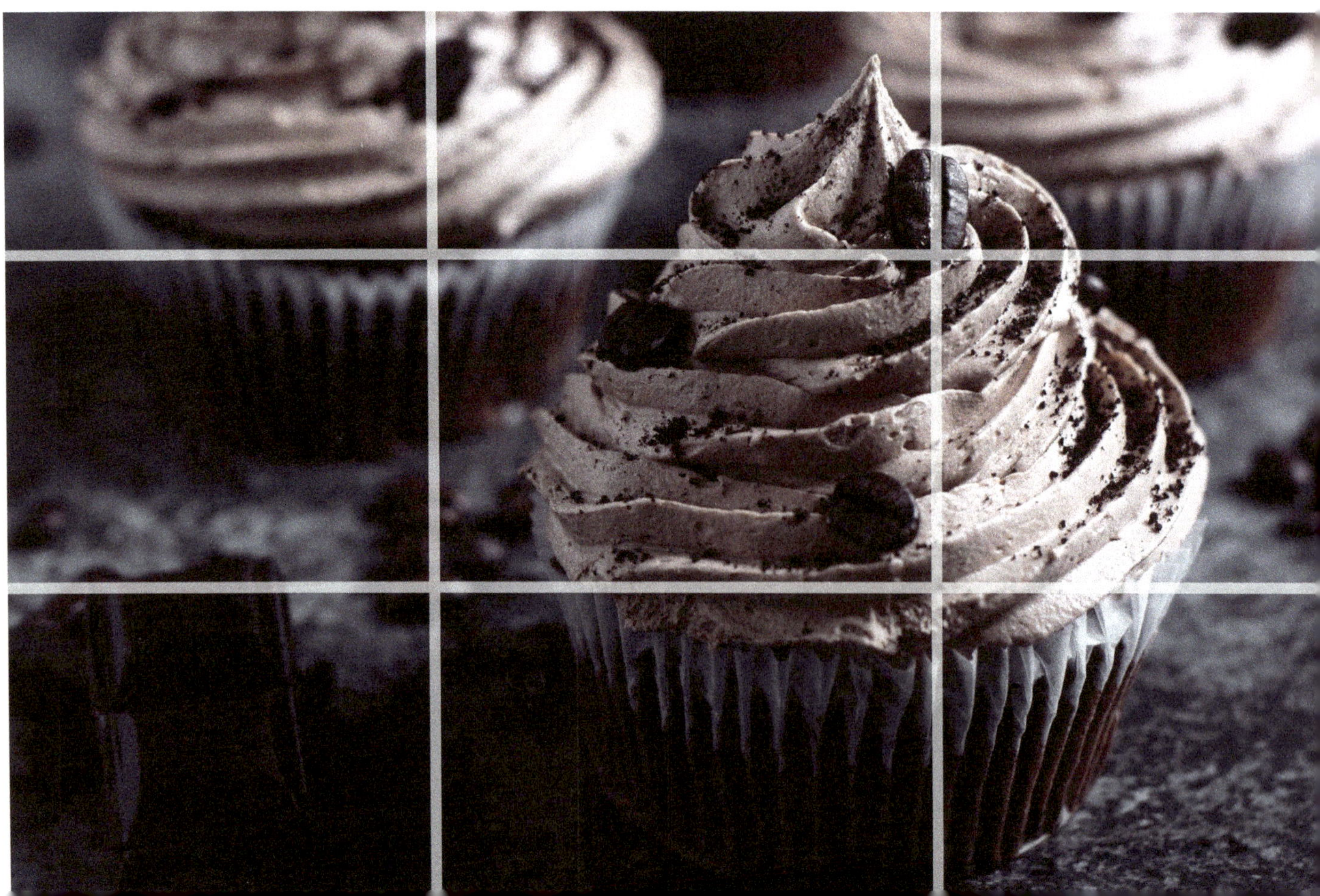

Too close or too far?

Capturing the detail in your dishes is important, it allows you to showcase all the wonderful effort you have put into decorating and styling your dishes. The details, however, are not the main event, they are part of the narrative. When selling your recipes, you want to use an image of the whole dish, this should be the first image the reader sees.

Zoomed in shots of the details or zoomed out shots of the whole table are important images for your blog post or website as they help with the narrative, they tell the story of your recipe but they are not the main event. When choosing what images to submit to recipe sites or to use for your social media links, you should choose images that show the whole dish as the main focus of the image. After all; your readers want to see what they will be making or eating.

Keep your horizon level

If you take away only one piece of advice from me, please remember to keep your horizons level. Some people fall into the trap of rotating their camera to create what they think will be an interesting composition. This technique was popular for food images in the '90s and like brown lipliner and overplucked eyebrows, it should be left there. It's just too confusing for the viewer and it makes your subject look strange. Please, please, and please, keep your horizon as level as possible.

Vertical or Horizontal?

When it comes to deciding the orientation of your images, it's mostly down to your taste. There are often multiple ways to photograph a scene and they all work, it's just down to you to experiment and find out what looks good to you.

There are some general rules to keep in mind, but in saying that, rules are made to be broken. If you're photographing something tall, it's wise to capture it vertically to get it all in the frame without having to shoot from far away. Similarly, if you're photographing something wide, horizontal is the best.

There are, however, times when this will not be possible when you have to stick to a particular orientation and your subject simply will not fit, you need to get creative. Will that long cheese board look good to shoot from above to keep the frame vertical?

Shooting from an Angle

Choosing the angle to shoot at is just as important as choosing where to place the subject in the frame. A flat pizza will be shot better from above rather than from a 90-degree angle as it has no depth and all the action is going on up top. Whereas if a sandwich is shot from above, it will look terrible because all you will see is bread.

Shooting from between 90 and 45 degrees will be best so you can see what's going on inside. When choosing a camera angle, you should have a good look at your subject, where are the focal points? Where's the action? Is your subject long? Tall or flat? Is your subject short, do you want to be thinking about more of a 45-degree angle to get it all in? Or tall and you can get away with 90 degrees to fit the whole subject into the frame.

Three Quarters

The three-quarter angle is particularly pleasing for food, this is because it best matches the angle from which you would naturally see food if you were sat at a table about to tuck in. This tends to be a universally flattering angle because you can see enough of both the front and the top of the dish.

This angle will work for a wide range of dishes and is particularly good for dishes inside a bowl. Bowls are difficult, because shooting from eye level is out of the question, as you won't see the food. However, not all dishes lend themselves to being shot from overhead. This leaves you with somewhere in the middle. By shooting at three-quarters you can clearly see the food.

Get Down to Eye Level

Sometimes you have to sink to the food's level, literally. Getting down to eye level is a great way to make food look taller. It's also essential when the food is only interesting from the side. Again, sandwiches and burgers are a great example of this, all the action is on the side. This angle is also great for drinks that don't have any garnishes or interest on the surface.

Get Overhead

Flat lay or overhead shots have skyrocketed in popularity over the past few years. This is definitely an angle to consider when you are planning your shoot. This angle is useful when you want to show a lot of elements at once. Overhead shots work best when your food is flat or at least not particularly tall. Having all of your elements at a similar height helps you keep the whole image in focus. Despite this, you can also get interesting shots using tall food, with only the top being in focus. Drinks with interesting garnishes are a great example of this.

Background and Foreground

When considering where to place objects within your frame, it's is equally as important to consider the objects in the background or foreground. These aspects can still play a significant part in your images. Objects placed in the background, are generally best left out of focus. Since they are not the focus of the image, they can be distracting. They don't need to be completely blurred out, but the focus should be soft enough that they do not distract from the main subject.

Another way to keep these additional elements from distracting the viewer is to position them in the corners of the frame. This creates a little distance between them and the main subject that they are not a distraction but far enough into the frame so that they are not looked over altogether.

These elements are added to the image to create a scene, you want them to hint at what's going on but you want the viewer to focus on the main dish. For example, when photographing a stack of pancakes, you may have a glass of orange juice in the background alongside an extra plate and some cutlery. This sets the scene of the image, creating the impression that you are just about to sit down for breakfast.

The extra elements that we add to our images help to tell the story.
The next time you are photographing a beautiful dish, think about who's eating it, where are they, what else are they eating/drinking? Create a little narrative in your head about who the food is for and try to set that scene within your image.

Groups of Three / Triangles

Have you ever noticed that in photographs, food is grouped in threes? Even in restaurants, appetizers are also served in threes? After working in restaurants for over 9 years, I can confidently tell you that this is not done to simply infuriate diners. Sure, it's definitely a consequence, but odd numbers are seen as being more appealing to the eye. Odd numbers are often used in interior design, apparently, there is something in our brain that is satisfied by seeing objects grouped in odd numbers.

You can replicate this in your food images by creating triangles and by grouping food in threes. By creating triangles, I don't mean that you have to carve out that burger into a triangle. I mean place items in the frame in a triangular shape so that if the viewer connected the dots, it would form a triangle. This technique helps the viewer navigate the image, instead of focusing on one element, their eyes are drawn from one element to the next, ending back at where they began, and hopefully, repeating the process. This helps them to take in the full image.

Adding groups of three to your images is simple. Instead of photographing 4 cupcakes, photograph three. This also works with garnishes, keep them in little groups of three around the scene. This will work for any types of garnishes from fruit to crumbs.

Finding Your Focal Point

Once you have set the scene, decided on the lighting, the props and have got the food looking fabulous, you need to decide where to put the focal point. An excellent place to start is at one of the intersecting points of the Rule of Thirds but this is not always true for every image.

If you're finding it difficult, experiment with a few different placements and see which you like best. Remember to keep the focal point on your main subject and you won't go too wrong. A good way to do this is to look at the image large on your computer screen and see where your eye is naturally drawn. This is probably the best place to put your focal point.

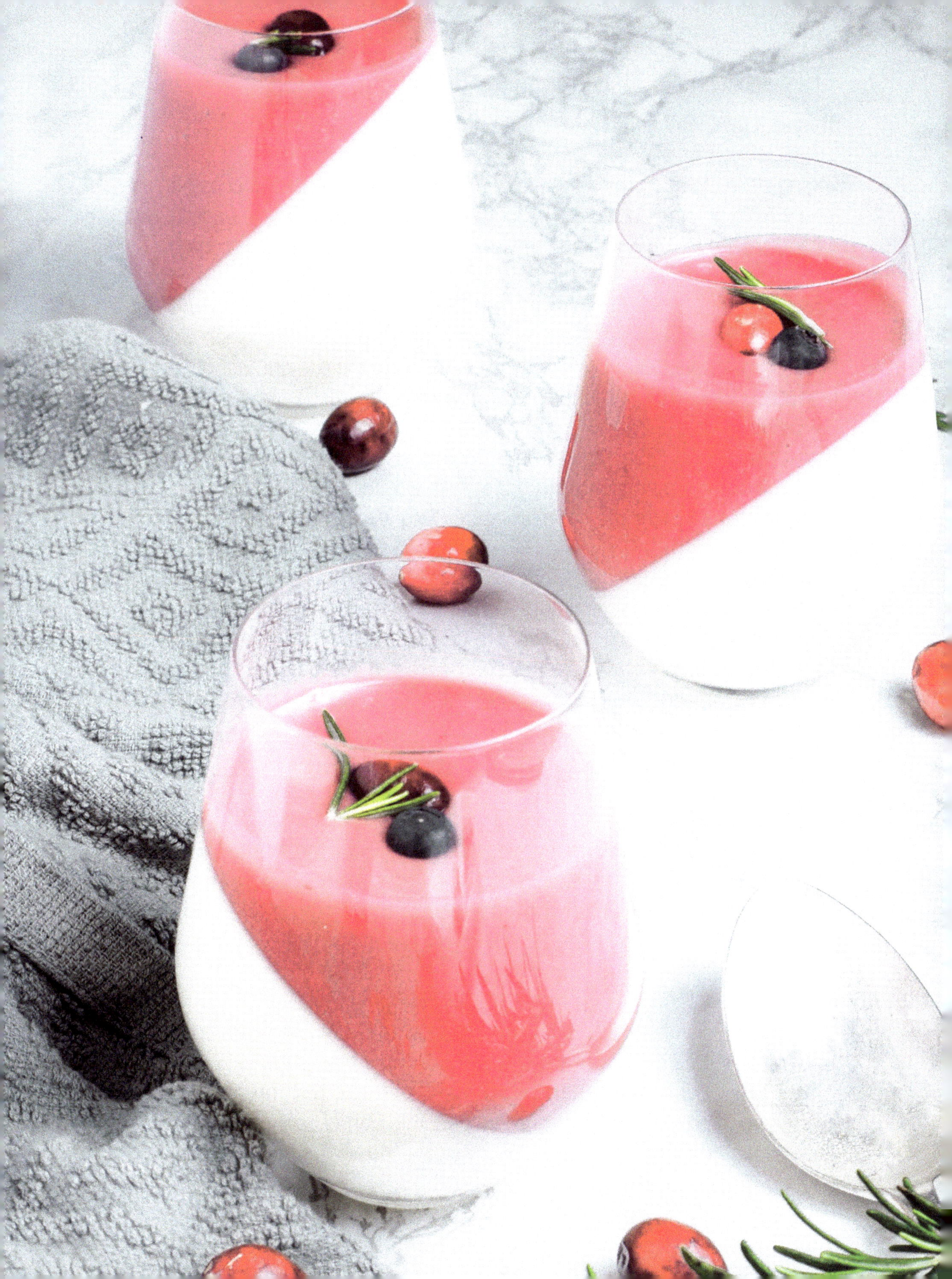

Shapes, Lines, and Colors

Paying close attention to the shapes, lines, and colors in your images will go a long way to helping you create beautifully balance images. These aspects affect the balance of the image and help the viewer when looking at your image.

Shapes

This is the main reason why square plates are difficult to photograph well in an image. They create harsh corners that are jarring to the eye and are often difficult to place. I like to stick to round crockery because they don't stand out and distract the viewer's eye.

If you have square food, for example, crackers, you would offset the harsh shape by stacking them overlapped and offset. This way, although the crackers themselves are square, the overall footprint they leave is not.

Leading lines

Leading lines are crucial in all types of photography, they are a way to draw the viewers eye to where you want them to go. Their eyes will naturally follow a line, so watch where your lines go. Lines can be created easily in food images with cutlery. Placing your silverware leading from the corner of the image to your food naturally draws the eye to your main subject. This technique works in all types of photography.

Color

Color plays an integral role in the way we look at food. There have been thousands of studies into the way our brain reacts to different colors in relation to food. Our eyes are naturally drawn to the brightest part of a photograph first, and this is often the color that is brightest or stands out the most.

If your main dish is mostly one color group, which most are, it is helpful to add another element in a contrasting color to help draw your viewers eye. For example, a bowl of spaghetti, which is in the red/yellow spectrum of the color wheel, would often be photographed with a sprig of basil. This pop of contrasting color grabs the viewers' attention.

When you photograph food, you want to highlight the main subject so that your viewer's eye is drawn there first, you don't want them to focus on other elements. Bright food or crockery in the background, that is brighter or more brightly colored than the main subject can be distracting and draw your viewers eyes to it instead.

Sometimes when you have food that doesn't have a lot of color, maybe it only has one prominent color, you can get excellent results from sticking to those colors. You can exaggerate this color by adding elements of the same color around it.

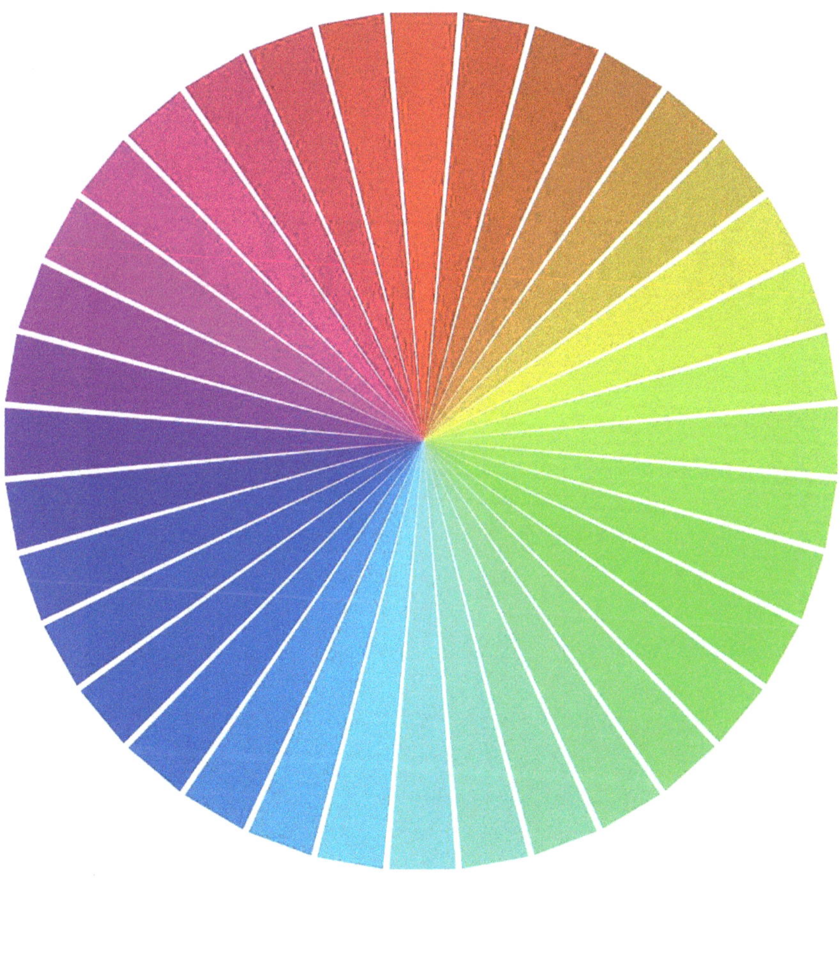

The Color Wheel

FOOD STYLING

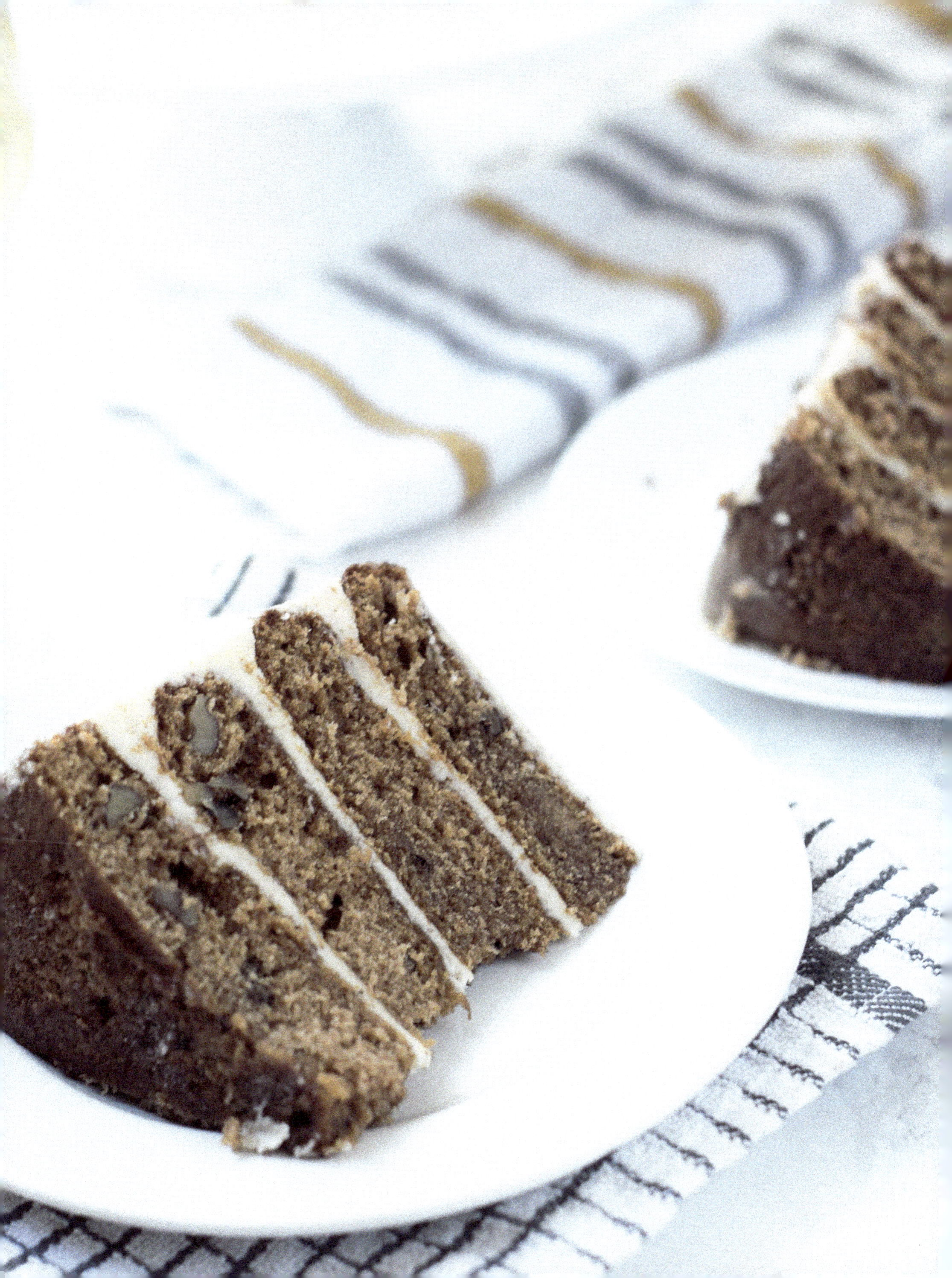

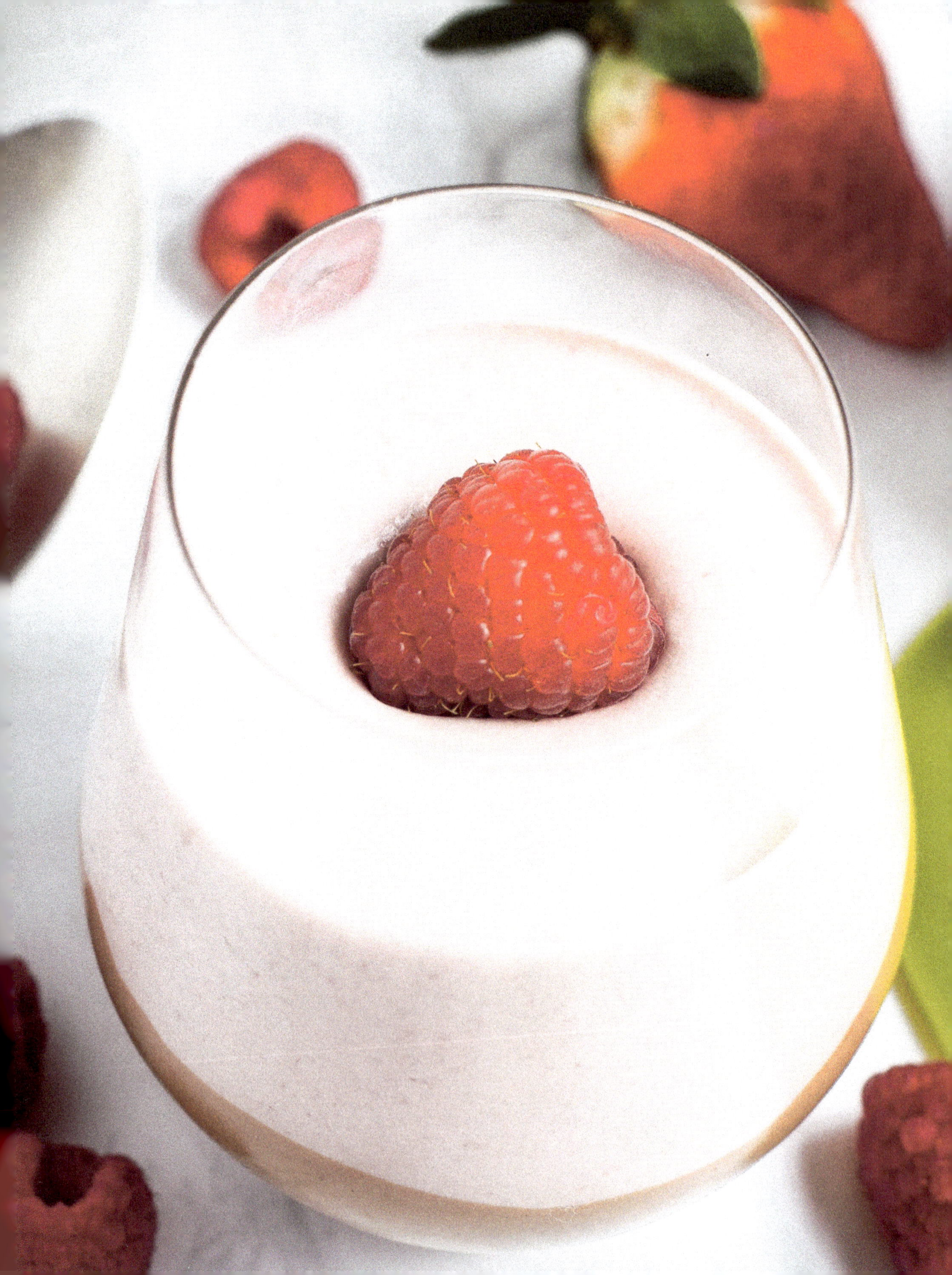

Introduction to Food Styling

When you delve into the world of food photography, you quickly learn that it is far more than grabbing some food and snapping away. The best food images often take hours of hard work by a whole team of people to capture. A food stylist is a professional whose job it is to make the food look amazing. Usually from a culinary background, food stylists are there to ensure that the dish looks its best for the camera.

Now, I understand that the average amateur photographer making images for themselves or for a blog cannot afford a food stylist. It's quite possible to do this yourself once you have a little know how. Food stylists employ a range of tips, tricks and techniques to get dishes to look delicious.

Food stylists understand that when we eat, we use all of our senses at once, we see the plate, we smell the food, we feel the texture in our hands or on our tongue and then finally we taste. How often have you been resistant to try a new dish because it didn't look appetizing?

Eating is a sensual experience and we as photographers have to try and convey that experience in a single photograph. It is our job to help our audience imagine the flavor of the dish, it's aroma and to bring out its unique texture.

In this chapter, I will walk you through the food styling essentials, props, backgrounds, surfaces, tools of the trade and all of the tips and tricks that food stylists employ to make dishes look delicious. You can try all of the tips or try out just a few. It's up to you.

Creating a beautiful food image is art and as long as you keep the experience in mind and try not to go all Picasso on me, I think you'll do just fine.

Tips and Tricks

Using stand-ins

Have you ever found yourself taking so long to set up your photograph that your food has gone cold and sad looking? Your herbs have wilted or your juicy steak has started to look more Saharan than sizzling? This is because all food has a life span, the moisture evaporates out, the hot lights melt it or it starts to congeal. This is completely normal, natural and a sign of fresh ingredients. But it isn't ideal.

In order to be able to take your time setting up and get everything just right, you need a stand-in. Much like in the movies, food photographers also employ stand-ins to help them get the shot set up perfectly before they put the food in.

A stand-in can be anything, an unused piece of food, or a cloth. As long as it represents about the same shape and size of what it's standing in for. A good tip is that if your food is white, like yogurt, use a white stand in. If your food isn't white, don't use a white stand in. This is because the presence of something white will dramatically change your meter reading.

Set your scene up with the stand in, get your lighting and props perfect. Then you can set your food up, replace the stand in with the real thing and start taking photos straight away. The food doesn't sit there and cool off while waiting for you to tweak the lighting.

Adding bulk

When working with liquid food like soups, cereals or saucy pasta, often, the chunks fall to the bottom of the bowl, leaving you to wrestle and try to get them to stay on the surface long enough to capture a photo. This is where a ramekin or smaller bowl comes into play. Adding another smaller bowl, turned upside down into your soup bowl will add volume, making the bowl appear fuller, and allow any decoration to sit on top; appearing as if they are floating on the surface of the soup.

This is a really old and well-used trick in food styling as solid food sinks when suspended in liquid. This is also a great way to make the bowl appear fuller when photographing things like pasta. The weight of the food has a tendency to make it squash down and the bowl does not look as full. Simply piling the food on top of the upside-down ramekin prevents it from sinking down to the bottom.

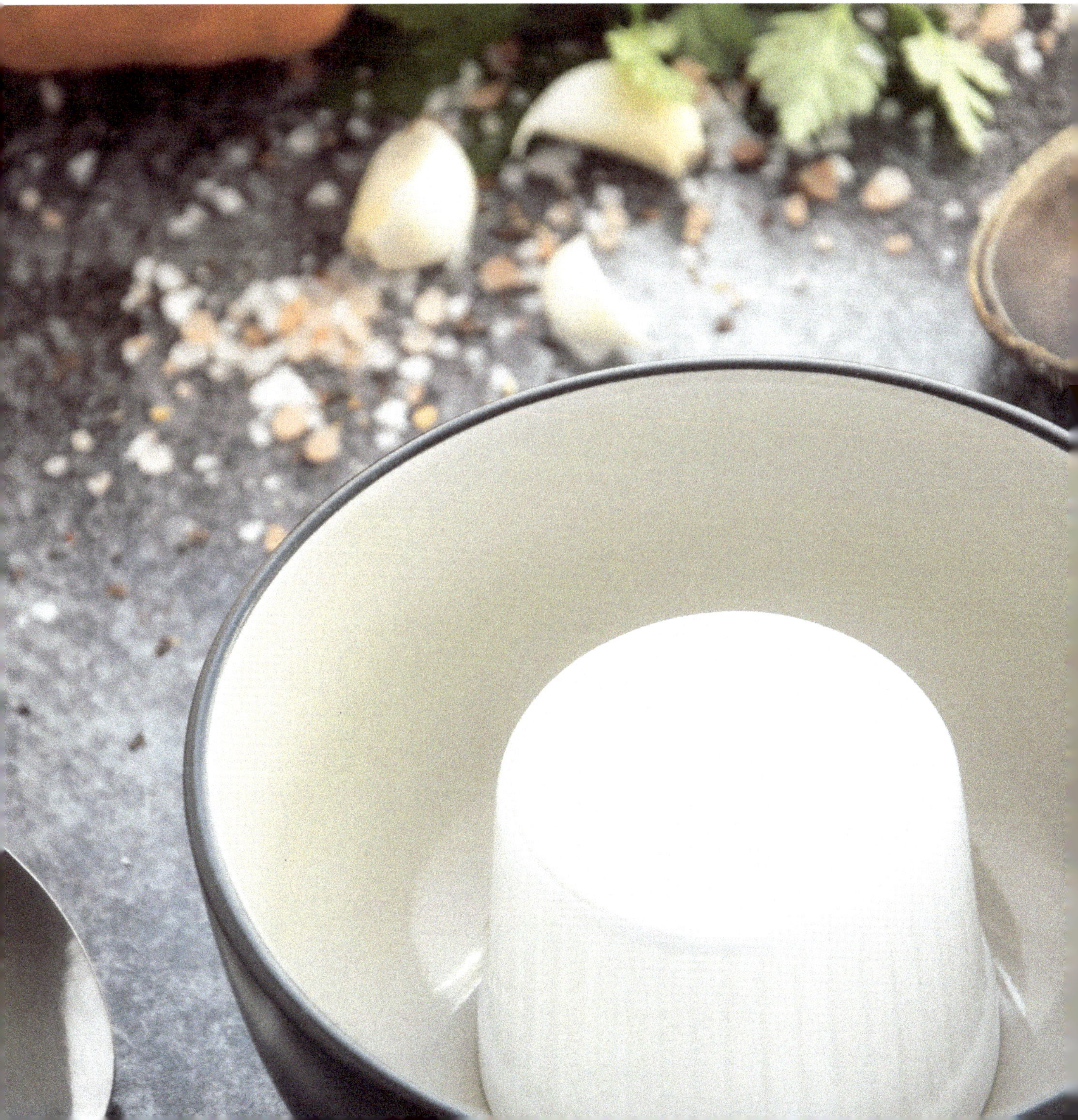

Flat food

When working with flat food, such as tortilla wraps or pancakes, often when we pile them up and there is very little distinction between the layers. To get that volume and that clear definition between layers, you can add another layer in-between. A piece of cardboard, folded paper towel or a smaller piece of food works great to give that subtle lift to the dish. Having a clear definition between the layers not only gives you a little extra height but help the viewer see exactly what it is they are looking at.

It's important to note that when working with flat food like this, it's always a good idea to shoot from between 40 and 90 degrees. No overhead shots. Shooting overhead will lose all perspective that you are looking at a stack.

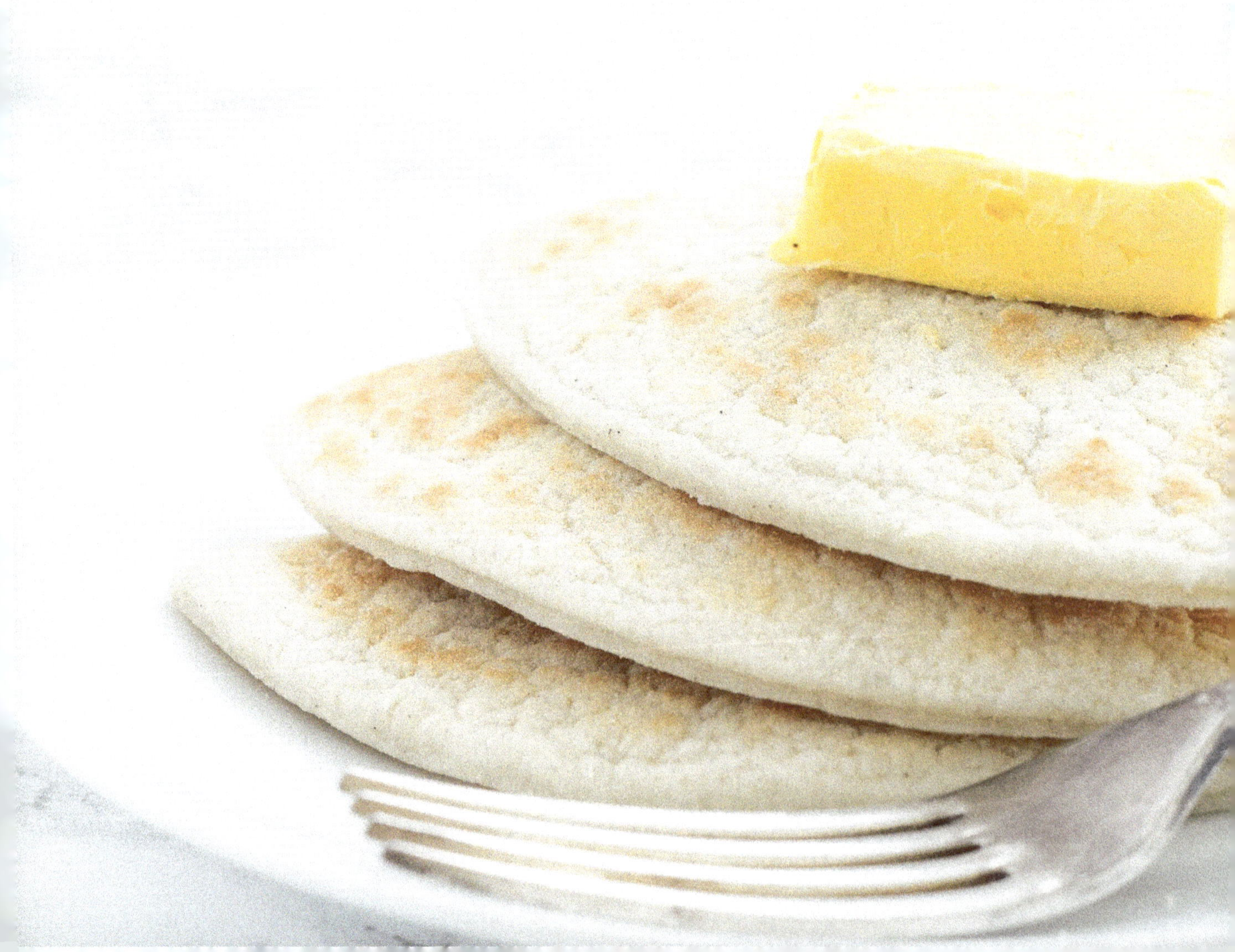

Garnishes

A good food stylist knows how to work garnishes to their advantage. Having an extra contrasting bright pop of color really lifts the image and adds interest. When choosing your garnishes, keep in mind the dish you are garnishing.

A beautiful Indian curry would look silly garnished with rainbow sprinkles. Try and choose a garnish that would be used in the dish. Curry would be garnished with chopped chili, coriander, limes or other similar spices that you would expect to have with a curry.

Make it messy

I am a great fan of a little mess in my images. Food is not always perfect and so you shouldn't expect every dish you photograph to be. A few crumbs sprinkled on the surface or sauce dripping down the side adds life to the image. It makes it look less staged and more like someone is about to sit down to enjoy the dish.

Especially if your photograph is going to sit alongside a recipe, a little mess makes the dish seem more attainable to the viewer. If it looks too done and perfect, they may see it as too difficult for them to make themselves.

Movement

Another way to add interest to your images is to add a sense of movement. Drizzling syrup over pancakes or having a fork full of food as if someone is taking a bite. This adds to the realism of the image.

Have a look at your dish and think about what movement would naturally happen. You could have a hand sprinkling salt or a pepper grinder sprinkling pepper grinds. There are endless opportunities available with each dish, you just have to get creative.

Using Fresh Ingredients

When you cook a delicious meal to eat yourself, you buy the freshest ingredients. So why would you use anything else in your food images? One of the ways of achieving beautiful looking food images is to purchase beautiful, fresh food. All fresh food has a relatively short lifespan and its freshness is already dwindling when you pick it up in the supermarket.

One of the ways to keep food fresh as possible is to purchase it on the day or the day before you intend to photograph it.

Once you get a feel for food photography and you've been going a few months, you will get a feel for what shops are best for what ingredients. Some stores will be best for meat and poultry but their veggies will look terrible. Others will have lovely fresh fruit and veg but their meat will suck. It will take you a while to get the lay of the land. For example, when I'm making a dish, I might go to three or even four stores to get my ingredients.

And while we're on the subject of fresh ingredients, it's generally best to use fresh over canned or frozen. Fresh food holds its shape much better when cooked. When frozen food is cooked; it tends to look mushy and the color is not as vibrant. It just looks a little sad.

There are a few exceptions to this, frozen peas, for example, hold their shape and structure just fine. Frozen fruit is another good example if you're going to be stewing or baking it. Although, frozen fruit is not good to use as a garnish.

Shopping Smart

Ingredients are expensive and whenever we're shopping, we should take care of what we place in our basket. The worst thing is to buy all of your ingredients, only to get them home and realize that they're not fresh or they've been squashed at the bottom of the grocery bags.

When shopping for ingredients, take your time to make sure that whatever you're putting into your basket is fresh, blemish and mold free. Yes, mold, I've lost count of the times I purchased some onions, only to get home to discover that they are moldy.

And when you've chosen your beautiful, blemish free, fresh produce, treat it with care. Don't just chuck it in the basket and hope for the best. Make sure that those berries don't get squashed. A good tip is to find a supermarket which lets you take cardboard produces boxes, you know the one's fruit and vegetables come in. Use these instead of plastic bags, not only will you help the environment but you will prevent your produce from getting squashed.

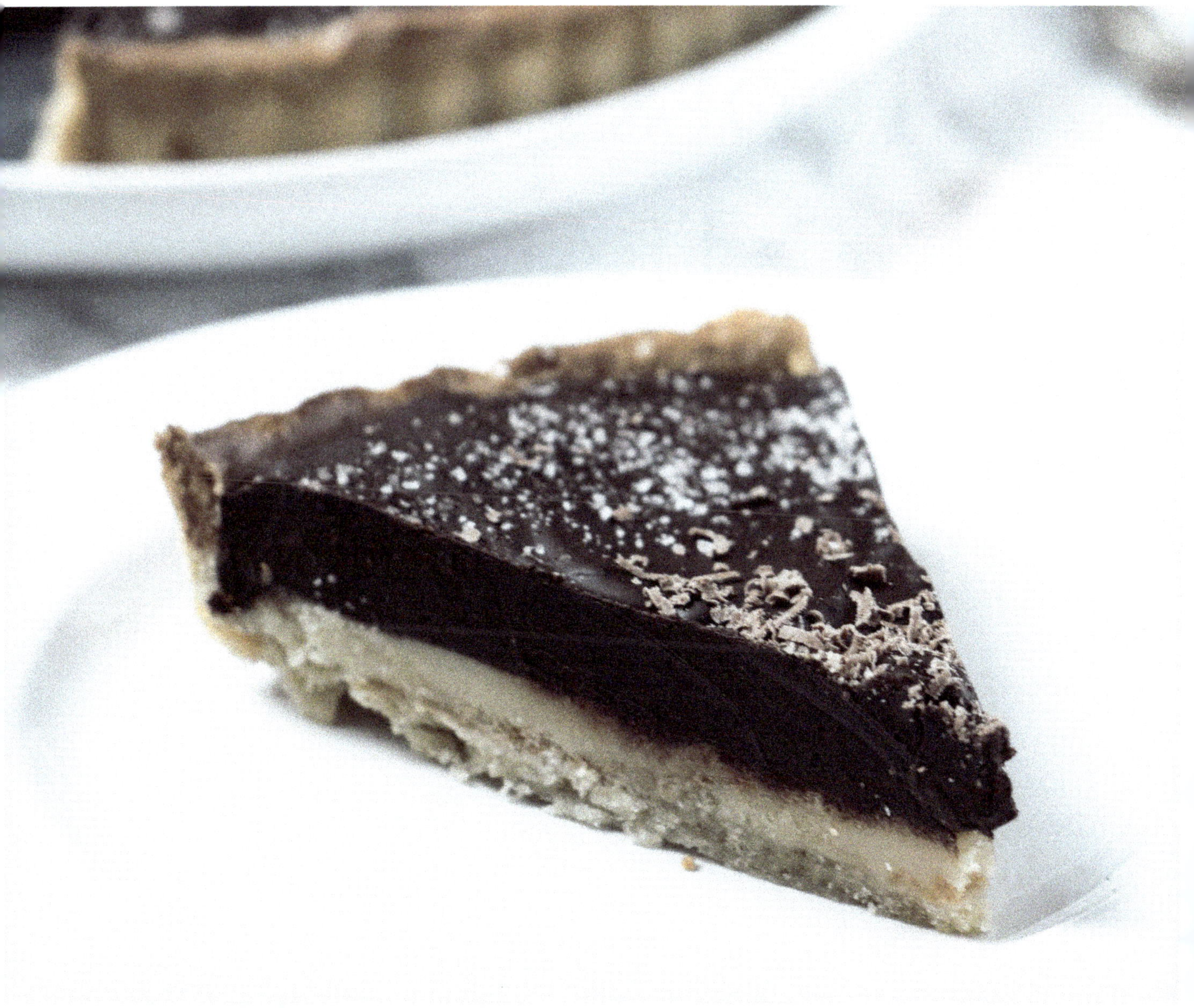

TOOLS OF THE TRADE

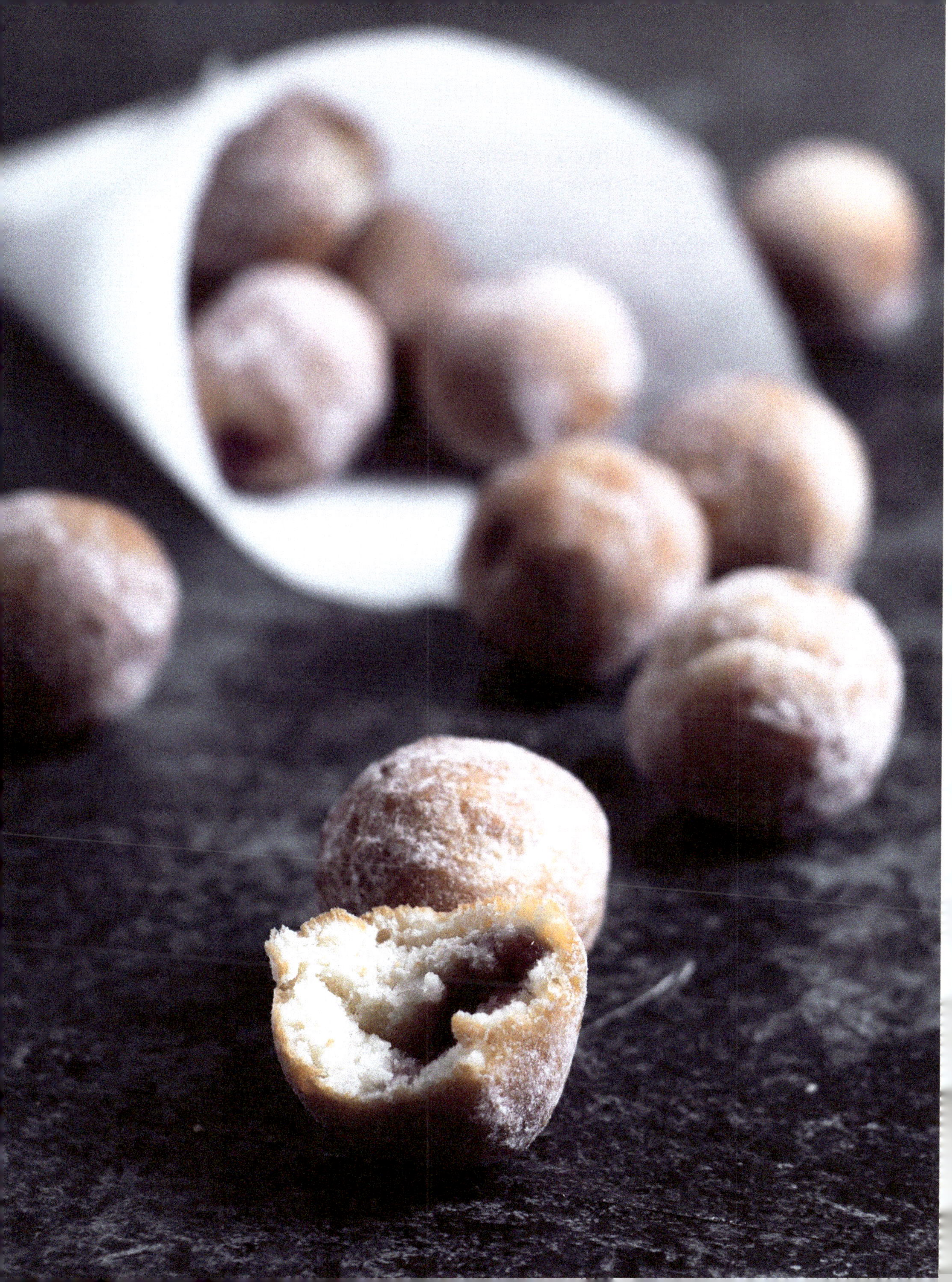

15 Must Have Food Styling Tools

Whether you're a food blogger on the weekends or a professional food photographer, at some point; you're going to have to get to grips with food styling. How you style your images is just as important as how you light the scene. Most professional food photographers work with a food stylist to ensure that the food is looking its best. However, if you're not so lucky to have someone to create the scene, you'll need to learn the tools of the trade.

Food stylists will have a whole arsenal of tools and equipment available to them to help them achieve results. With just a few essential tools, you can easily achieve the same results at home. Most of these tools can be purchased cheaply and are easy to find. With the exception of a few higher priced items.

What to include in your food styling kit

1. Paper Towels

Spillages are going to happen; you're going to get sauce on your beautiful white plate. Accept that the universe is imperfect and plan for the inevitable. Paper towels are cheap and easy to grab for a quick touch up. However, not all paper towels are made equal. I like to buy the Bounty brand paper towels as they are a low lint option. If you're working with a macro lens or with dark crockery, the last thing you need is to take an amazing photo, only to spend hours editing all of the fluff out.

2. Q-tips

Another clean up essential is the humble Q-tip. Amazing for those tiny clean up jobs or getting into tight spaces. Again, not all Q-tips are made equal, opt for the cone-shaped ones that come to a fine point. And please, for the environment's sake, use the ones with a cardboard tube.

If you're struggling with lint, a great alternative to Q-tips are disposable lipstick applicators. They can be bought from beauty supply stores or online. They are completely lint-free and you can buy in bulk. Technically, they can be washed and re-used with a little dish soap.

3. Makeup Brushes

Makeup brushes are fantastic for dusting away crumbs or stray powdered sugar. I like fan brushes or small eye shadow brushes. As long as they are small and fluffy, they will work great. You don't need to spend much cash on these. If your local dollar store has a cheap brush set, it will work great too. You just need something that will gently sweep away any unwanted fluff, dust or crumbs.

4. Makeup Application Sponges

Have you noticed that a lot of these tools are make-up tools? Don't be using your expensive beauty blender for this. I'm talking about those cheap wedge-shaped sponges that you can get in bulk. These are fantastic for holding food in place and propping things up. They can be cut down to size and easily hidden so the camera can't see them. They're great for flat lays when you need things to sit at a different angle.

5. Tweezers

Tweezers come in all shapes and sizes and they're all lifesavers for food styling. If you're just starting out, don't go out and buy expensive culinary tweezers. Regular cheap tweezers will work just fine as well. Later, when you want to expand your food styling toolbox, you can look into culinary tweezers. Tweezers are great for when you need to remove something small from the plate without disturbing the rest of the scene.

6. Museum Putty

Blu Tack or white museum putty is fantastic as a food styling tool. It's reusable and reliable and has so many different uses. It prevents items from rolling or sliding, prop items up or stick things down. Trust me, after years of photographing food, I still surprise myself and find new uses for museum putty all the time.

7. Tooth Picks / T Pins

Toothpicks and T-pins come in handy when you're trying to build height with your food. If you're stacking a burger, sandwich or even pancakes. If you're struggling to maintain height, you need something to keep it all together. I like to have both toothpicks and T-pins because they are good for different things. You can break toothpicks up into smaller pieces to hold smaller things together, like the edges of wraps. T-pins are thinner and smoother than toothpicks, so, they don't disturb the food that much when inserted.

8. Spray Bottles

Those tiny little spray bottles you usually get in travel sets are so unbelievably useful in food photography. There's a number of things that you would need to spray over your food and I always recommend 4 spray bottles. I always have 1 filled with water, another with a glycerine mix, one with light oil and another with ascorbic acid. More on ascorbic acid later. The fine mist these bottles produce is perfect for just getting the mist where you want it. Larger bottles produce a heavy spray that's going to get everywhere and coat everything.

9. Paint Brushes

Those cheap art sets from the dollar store are great for this. Sometimes in life, and in food photography, you have to cheat. Paint brushes are fantastic if you have less than appetizing meat that you need to brown with Kitchen Boquet. They are also great for painting on sauce, food coloring or any other fine detail that literally need to be painted on your dish.

10. Heat Gun

Heat guns and blowtorches both come into this category and are one of the only things on this list you probably can't get from the dollar store. They perform different tasks. Heat guns are used for gently melting and for getting the cheese on a burger to just soften. They can take the frosty look from frozen items and are primarily used when you just need a uniform, gentle heat. A kitchen blow torch is most useful whenever you need a blast of heat. Blow torches will burn food quickly...so use sparingly. They are used for things like caramelizing the sugar on a crème brulee.

11. Squeeze Bottles / Syringe

For the times when you need precise placement of sauces. Squeeze bottles and syringes are ideal for when you need sauce in a specific place. Syringes are needed to get into tiny spaces. They're also great for decorating plates, you can squeeze out a single dot of liquid and get really artistic with your decoration.

12. Ascorbic Acid

Ascorbic acid prevents fresh fruits and vegetables from oxidizing. Oxygen in the air causes a reaction in the fruit/vegetables causing them to go brown. You can either mix ascorbic acid with water in a spray bottle and coat the fruit/veg that you want to stay fresh or mix with water and simply dip the fruit into it.

13. Rubbing Alcohol

Rubbing alcohol is fantastic for cleaning before your shoot. It removes all grease, dirt, and dust. It also evaporates really quickly, so there's no need to dry the items.

14. Funnel

When you photograph drinks, smoothies or anything that needs to go into a glass, it's really difficult to get the liquid into the glass without it splashing up the sides. Once you have a splash, it is very hard to remove it, especially from the glass as the spot smudges and wreaks havoc. So that you don't have to start getting your Q-tips out, next time you're photographing something in a glass, try pouring it in with a funnel to avoid splashes.

15. Waterproofing Spray

I know, I've saved the most ridiculous one for last. You know the kind of aerosol fabric waterproofing spray you would use to spray on your shoes to stop water form soaking through? Well, you can use it to spray on food, stop sauces, liquid, and syrups from soaking in. The best example is with pancakes, normally when you pour syrup on pancakes, you would get the syrup soaking in on the top thereby creating a dark patch and not much drizzle. Coating the pancakes with this allows the syrup to run straight off the pancakes without soaking in, creating that perfect drip.

Props

Just as important as the food styling, is the prop styling. Choosing the correct props to suit the feel of the image is essential. The props you choose can have a huge impact on the image so take care when choosing your props.

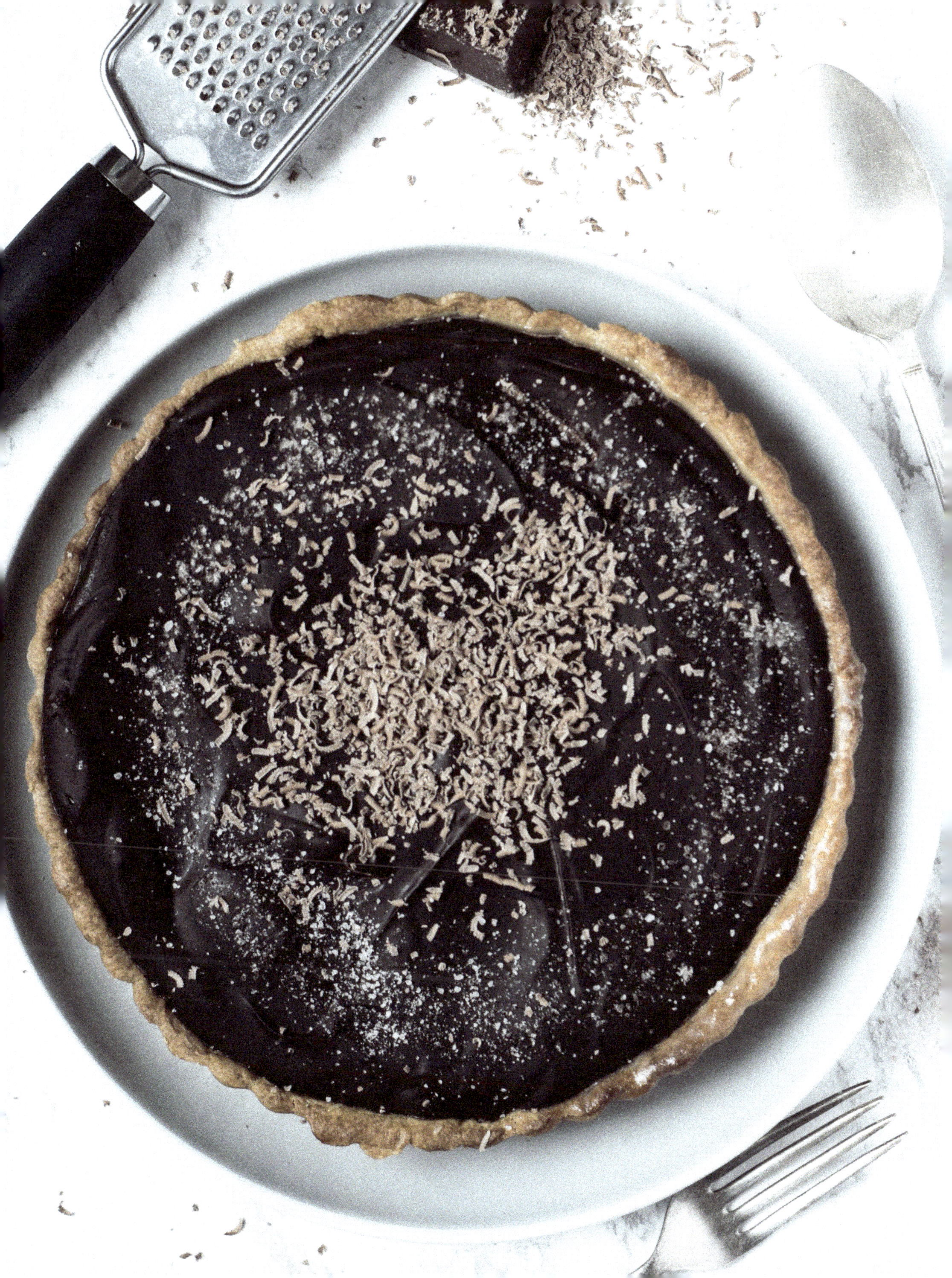

Props

I'll be the first one to admit that I have a serious shopping problem. Now, I don't buy clothes, shoes or bags, I have cupboards, shelves and closets full and bursting with food photo props. I have a serious problem; I can't help myself. I get all excited when I find interesting new props. My boyfriend, on the other hand, has a meltdown every time he has to get something out of a cupboard for fear of an avalanche.

Props can make or break an image and there are a lot of options available. So you don't end up like me, buried under an endless supply of cooling racks and napkins. I've devised a list of the essentials you need to start out, a list of basics you can mix and match to get the most out of your images.

There are two options for buying props, you can buy them new or second hand. Buying new props is fantastic because you can find exactly what you want, and there won't be any compromises. Buying new props, however, can be expensive. The market for affordable beautiful kitchenware has expanded dramatically in the past five years and you can find beautiful options in supermarkets and cheaper stores. In fact, I think there's almost no need to spend that much on kitchenware anymore at all.

Stores like TJ Maxx, Ikea and supermarkets make shopping for new kitchen props more affordable than ever. If you want to look at more expensive options, Habitat, John Lewis and Wayfair have some really beautiful option at the moment.

Prop shopping really gets interesting when you decide to buy second hand. There really isn't a replacement for a beautiful vintage piece. Ebay is an acceptable option but I've found that is has been getting more and more expensive for interesting kitchenware. The best finds are always found at car boot sales, garage sales, flea markets, and charity shops. These are where the most exciting finds are and where the best bargains can be found.

The downside to vintage finds is exactly that, they are finds. You will almost never find what you're looking for when you're looking for it. You usually have to live with what you get, but that's the fun of it.

Cutting Boards

You need at least one interesting cutting board. Realistically, I think three is optimum, a white marble, black marble or slate, and a wooden board. These three will be suitable for most images but there are hundreds of options available. Personally, I like unusual options like raw wood or something with an interesting shape. Cutting boards can also serve as a background or a surface to put your food on. They can be popped in the background to break up a horizon or placed just sneaking into an image to remove unwanted negative space.

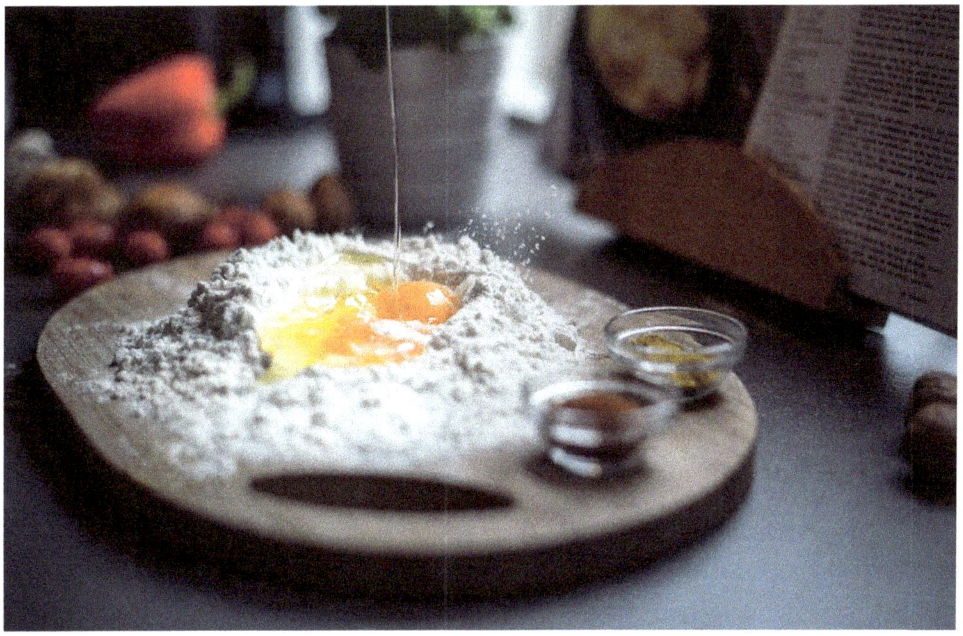

Cloths and Napkins

Cloths and napkins are by far my favorite prop to buy. They come in every conceivable color and they're easy to store. So you don't have to take up so much precious space, my suggestions would be to have mostly neutral and nude colors which always look good. Then you can throw in a few different colors and textures as you need them. Hessian or sackcloth is also a great option to give your image a rustic feel.
The texture is really important to look out for in your cloth and napkins. If you can get your hands on a cloth with an interesting texture, it can look wonderful in the right light.

Crockery

Crockery is something every budding food photographer needs to have and it's so easy to go crazy and buy everything you see. I f you are on a low budget, I don't think you can go wrong with plain, matte, white crockery. You can add some color to your images with some bright cloth or bright food. If you want a few more options, I'd say go for something in matte black and matte grey. I like to stay away from bright crockery, I think they can distract you from the food or end up looking too much when you look at the whole image. Bright crockery needs to be used carefully and with consideration.

To get started, you need some small serving bowls, some side plates, dinner plates and a couple of bowls. Maybe a large serving dish if you think you will need it. So, you can see how quickly your kitchen cupboards will start to fill up.

Utensils

Vintage utensils are my favorite! They look so beautiful and really make all the difference in your image. With utensils, you really don't need much and vintage cutlery doesn't even need to match. A couple of teaspoons, tablespoons, knives, and forks is all you need to start with. Knives and cake slices are also a great option.

If you don't like the look of vintage cutlery, there are lots of beautiful modern options available at the moment. I would go with interesting shapes or colors as it's easy for plain cutlery to blend into the background. Gold and rose gold cutlery are a great option as they really bring a modern feel to images.

Pans

Pots and pans are always a good idea to have when you cook, but making use of them in your images may have never occurred to you. Pans like copper or cast iron bring real interest and make a wonderful feature for your images. With regards to normal pans, I like a rustic, beat up, old pan from a garage sale, they really look interesting when photographed.

If you ever come across real copper pans on your hunt for vintage kitchen props, never walk away from them, they are kitchen gold dust!

Glasses

If you're planning on posting drinks recipes, you're going to need glasses. My suggestion is to get plain glasses as cut glass or patterned glasses can distract or even block your beverage. If you want to save on space, you can get away with only buying 2 of each kind of glass. I would suggest big wine glasses something that will suit both white and red wine. It will look strange having a huge pinot bowl with white wine in it. Champagne flutes, highball glasses, and whiskey glasses are also staples to have in the cupboard. I also love stemless wine glasses; they look great with liquid in them but also double up for use with mousses or any kind of dessert you would serve in a glass.

Cups

Cups are another necessity if you want to produce some hot drink recipes or photographs. They also come in handy when you are photographing something like cookies or anything you would dip in a coffee. A few basic cups will usually do and it is generally best to stick to plain cups, colors are fine but keep the bright patterns to a minimum.
Again, odds are you won't need a full set of mugs. So places like IKEA where you can buy cups cheaply and individually are great.

Cooling Rack

Cooling racks are very versatile in your images, you can pop them in the background or foreground to add some interest. You can also shoot your food directly on them. Mostly, I would recommend just using the one you have at home, but if you don't have one, buying a basic black cooling rack will suffice. If you want something really nice, I have two gold cooling racks, a square, and a round one and I love them, especially on a dark background.

Bakeware

You may not think it but your bakeware cupboard is a treasure trove of props. Anything you would make your recipe in can act as a prop All of your baking dishes, pans, tins, and trays can be used as props and surfaces. Vintage, rustic looking bakeware is great. But if you can't find anything vintage or you just want a different feel for your images, you can buy new bakeware. I would stick to neutral colors to start with and to save space.

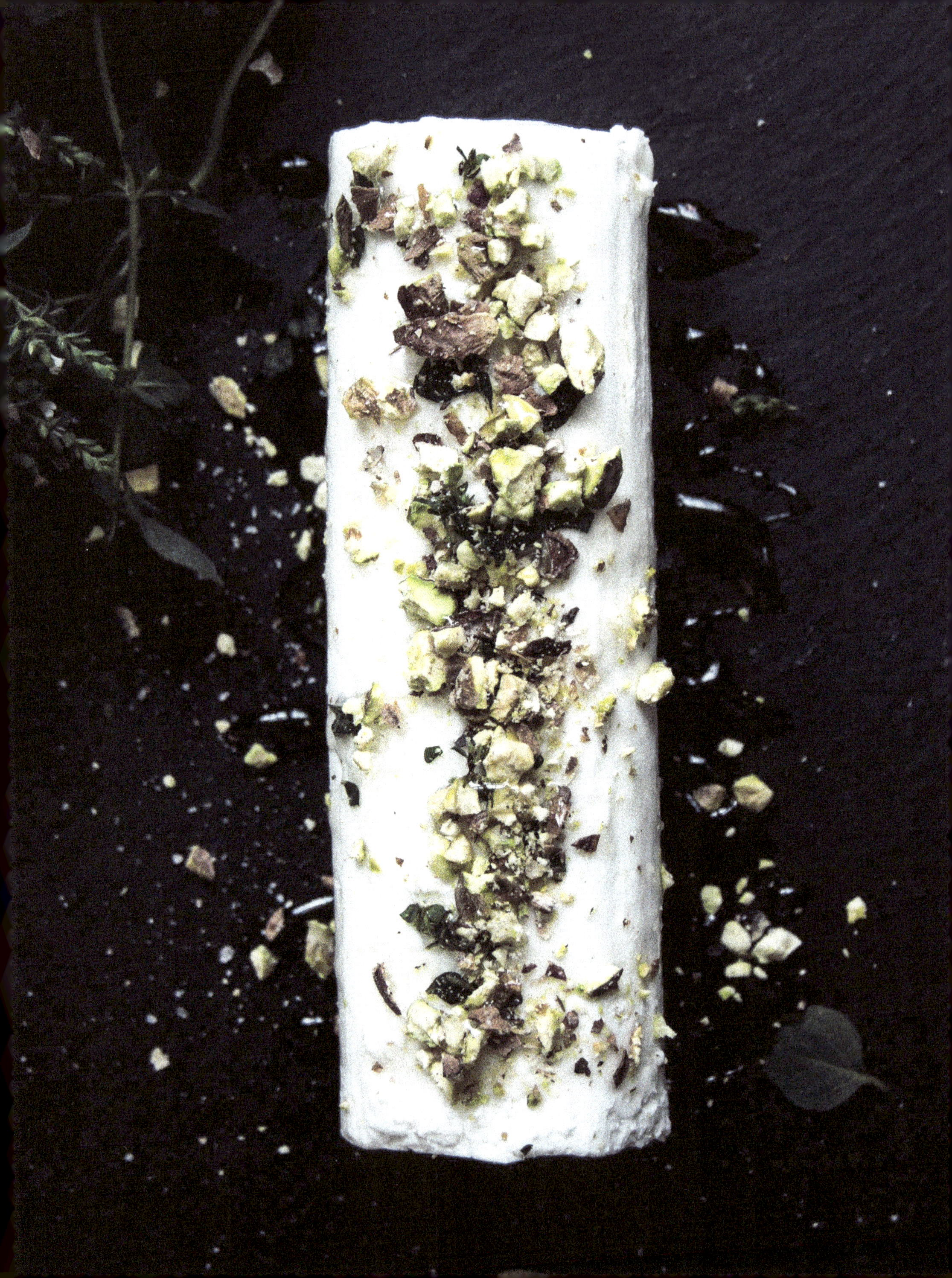

Backgrounds and Surfaces

When taking food images, we often focus too much on our subject. Although the food that we are photographing is without a doubt the most important aspect of the image, often, it is the other elements in the image that make it. Your choice of surface, background, and props can turn your image from average to amazing. Adding interest and context to your images, the backgrounds and props you choose are integrally important to your image.

When choosing your background, you have a whole host of options available to you. All of which depends on factors such as the space you have, the amount of money you want to spend and the effect you are trying to make.

Purchasing a background

If you are looking to purchase a ready-made background, there are a number of options available. The most popular of which would be a plain paper roll, most paper backgrounds come in very large rolls and need to be suspended on stands. They are quite large and take up quite a lot of space. If you have space, however, they are very versatile and useful. They are large enough to fit several people in the image. So it will be large enough to fit any food scene you can think of. The advantage of it being paper is that you can tear it off at the bottom if the paper gets tatty and you can tear it off and use the paper for something else.

PVC Rolls

Rolls of backgrounds are also available in PVC, some of which have been pre-printed with a background scene. My favorite of these are stone and brick wall effect. But you can get them in every imaginable form. The benefit to these is that because they are PVC, they are wipeable, which is a godsend when you are working with food. These rolls tend to be smaller than large paper rolls and easier to store and you don't need too much space to put it up. As with the paper rolls, you will also need two stands and a pole to suspend between the two. If you don't mind and you don't have a stand, you can pin or blue tack the background to a wall.

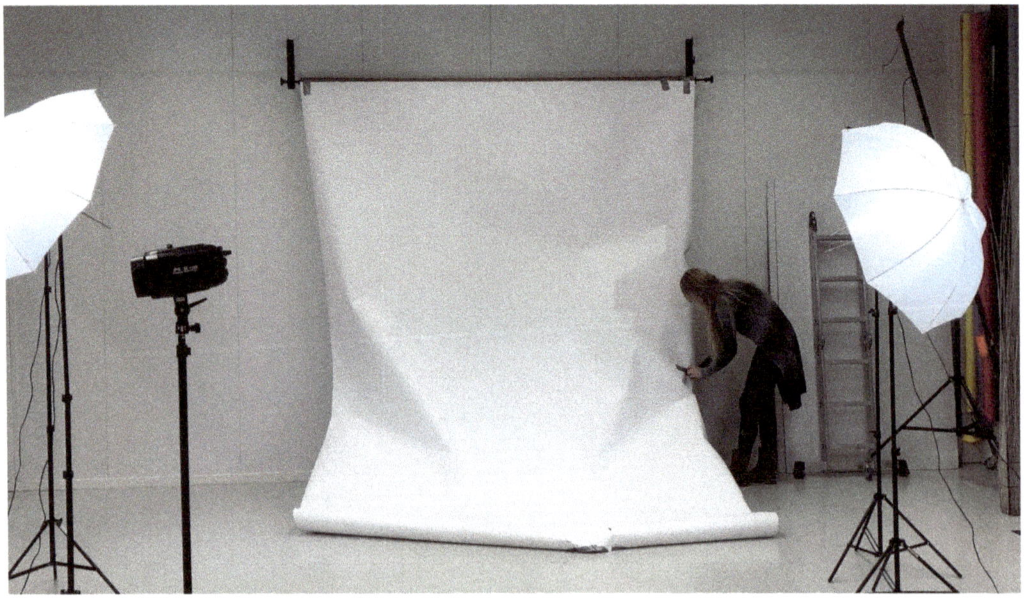

Fabric rolls

Another roll option would be fabric, although fewer options are available when compared to PVC, you can still get fabric backgrounds in a variety of different patterns. The benefit of fabric over PVC is that the fabric absorbs the light whereas the PVC will reflect the light and can prove problematic. They can also be unrolled and popped in the wash if you get food all over them. Again, you will need stands and poles to put the backdrop up but you can often find full kits which include stands for reasonable prices. I enjoy fabric backgrounds because you can cut a strip off the bottom of them and have a matching cloth in your image which is always a nice touch.

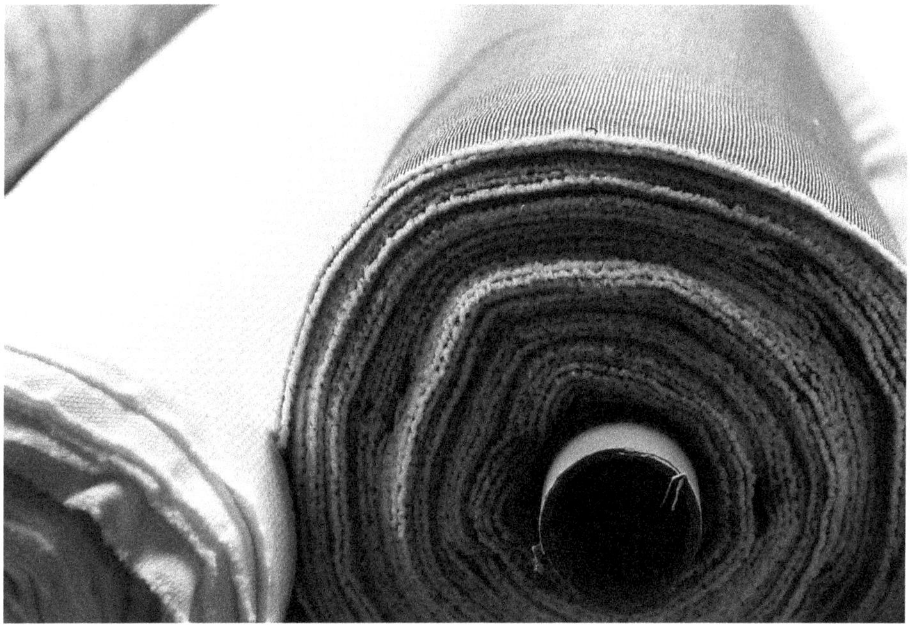

Other things you will need

As mentioned before, to use these purchased backgrounds; you will need a few things which includes: a stand and poles to hang the rolls, you will also need background clips to keep the background from unrolling and in the case of PVC or fabric backgrounds, you will either need a steamer or an iron with a steam capacity. This is because after some use, you will probably get creases in the background and they are often made from materials that you cannot use an iron on. Gentle steam will usually get the creases out.

Pop up backgrounds

If you do not have space for a full roll of background, there are several pop-up versions available. These pack away very small and spring to full size when you want them. You can then easily prop them up behind your subject and you have a small, portable background. The disadvantage to these is that quality pop up backgrounds tend to be expensive and they do not come in nearly as many patterns. You tend to get black, white and grey, then a few printed varieties. But if you are short on storage space, it is an option to look into. One of the best advantages is that the black and white pop up backgrounds can be used as reflectors and to block out the light when not in use as a background. So you get two functions for one price.

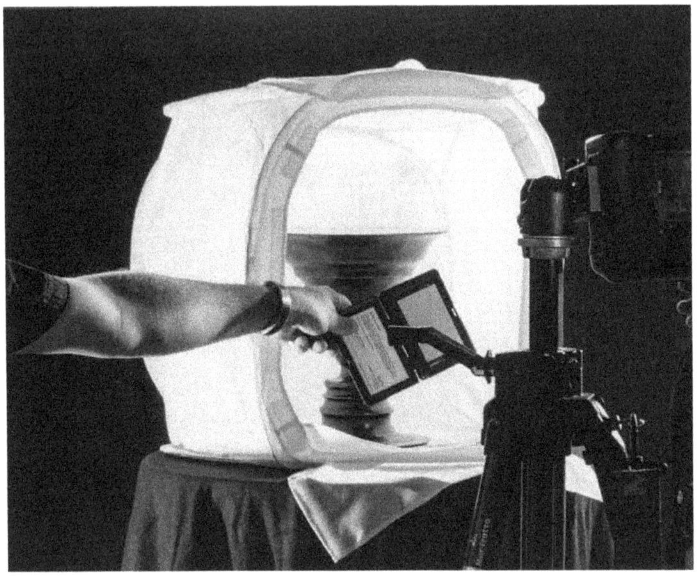

Portable options

Portable photo studios are also available to purchase. These are lightweight fabric boxes that can be put up anywhere. They need to be assembled next to a window or you need to shine your lights directly through the fabric but they work quite well. The disadvantage is that you can only have a white background. But if you shoot a lot of food on white backgrounds, they are worth looking into.

DIY Backgrounds

Of course, if you need something specific from your background or you need to keep costs down, there are far more DIY options available. In fact, the options are almost endless. The options for DIY backgrounds grow less and grow more expensive the larger you need them to be, but the advantage of a DIY option is that you can tailor it to be exactly what you need it to be.

I will start on DIY options with the most expensive. There are a number of online companies that will print images onto vinyl posters that are designed as large signature. There are a whole host of size options available to print on and you can have whatever you like printed onto them. The most well-known of these companies is Vista Print. If you want something very specific, you can use stock photo companies and purchase a photograph to have printed and use it as a background. If you are less picky and need to keep costs down, there are a number of websites that provide free, royalty free images.

The advantages to this are that you can get exactly what you want printed on the vinyl banner. It is also wipeable and easily folded away for storage. You will, however, need some way to hang it, you can either tack it to the wall or hang it from stands.

If you do not want to print on vinyl, you can do the same and print on paper. Prints can be made up to A0 from most printing companies which are quite a considerable size. The disadvantage of this is that paper is not cleanable and can get tatty quite quickly. If you don't need a large background this can be an excellent option.

Sticky back plastic

An excellent option for keeping costs down is sticky back plastic. A variety of different patterns are available and you can mount the plastic on a thin wooden board with little effort. These boards, being thin can be stored relatively easily and can also be used as surfaces to shoot on.

Vinyl film is available in a variety of different patterns including marble, wooden and stone. But there is a limit to the different types of film that can be bought. So, if you go this route, you will have to take what you can get. But I have found many excellent options with this and I myself have many vinyl covered boards.

Plywood

The same thin plywood that you can stick vinyl to can also very easily be painted and used in the same way. The advantage of this is that you can have one board that you paint and repaint depending on what you need. Water-based paint dries overnight so you can paint your background the night before and have it ready by the morning.

Wallpaper

One of my favorite photography finds of all time is wooden wallpaper. I have never particularly liked wallpaper. I had no idea that stone, wood and all kinds of interesting wallpaper existed. You can often get it very cheaply, so it is very easy to cut off and stick up.

With a whole range of different wallpaper available, I would advise any budding food photographer to browse their local DIY shop to see what they stock. These wallpapers can be used both as backgrounds and surface and, because they are inexpensive, it doesn't matter if you get food all over it.

Sticky back plastic

An excellent option for keeping costs down is sticky back plastic. A variety of different patterns are available and you can mount the plastic on a thin wooden board with little effort. These boards, being thin can be stored relatively easily and can also be used as surfaces to shoot on.

Vinyl film is available in a variety of different patterns including marble, wooden and stone. But there is a limit to the different types of film that can be bought. So, if you go this route, you will have to take what you can get. But I have found many excellent options with this and I myself have many vinyl covered boards.

Plywood

The same thin plywood that you can stick vinyl to can also very easily be painted and used in the same way. The advantage of this is that you can have one board that you paint and repaint depending on what you need. Water-based paint dries overnight so you can paint your background the night before and have it ready by the morning.

Wallpaper

One of my favorite photography finds of all time is wooden wallpaper. I have never particularly liked wallpaper. I had no idea that stone, wood and all kinds of interesting wallpaper existed. You can often get it very cheaply, so it is very easy to cut off and stick up.

With a whole range of different wallpaper available, I would advise any budding food photographer to browse their local DIY shop to see what they stock. These wallpapers can be used both as backgrounds and surface and, because they are inexpensive, it doesn't matter if you get food all over it.

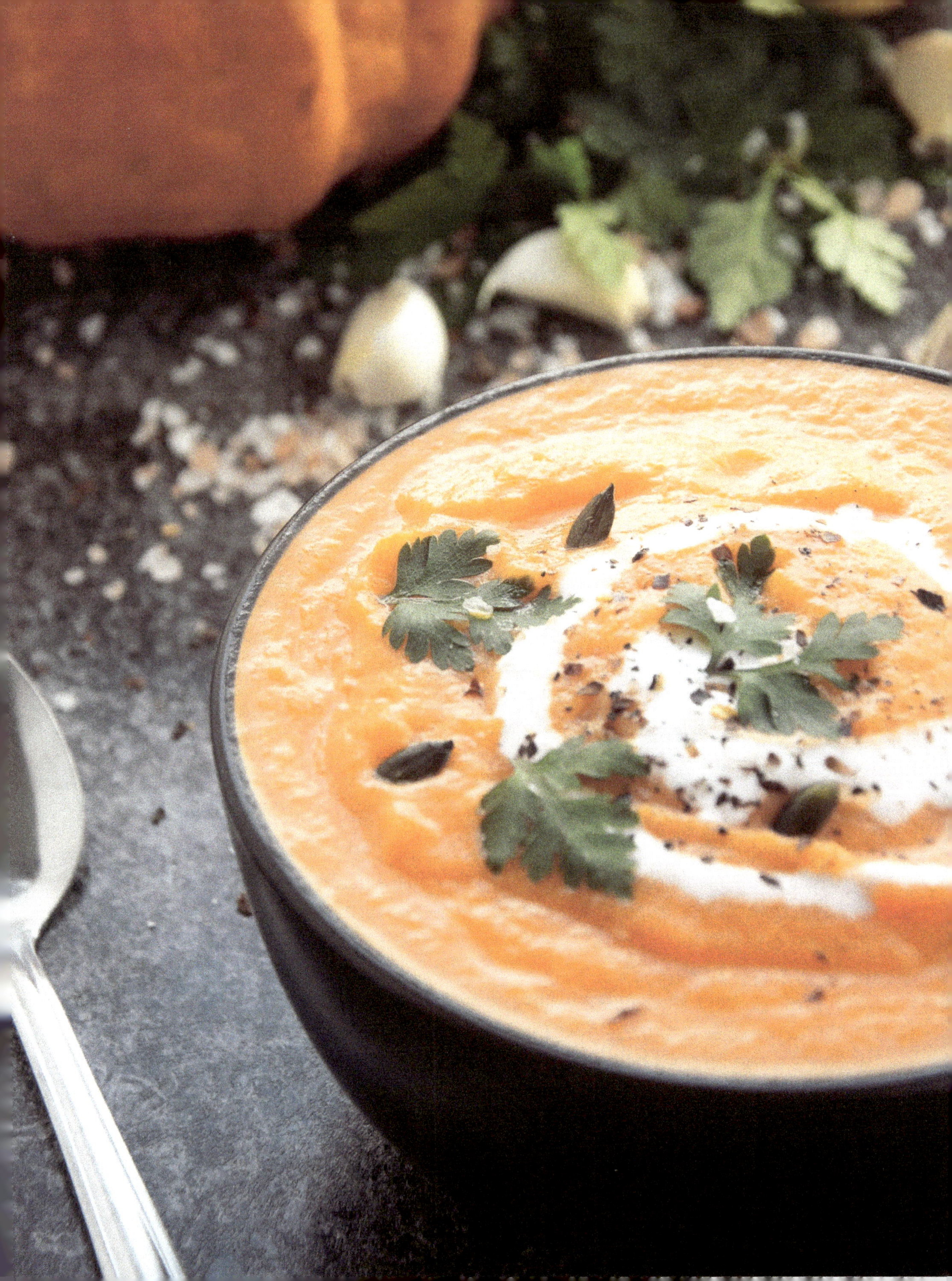

Now, PUT IT ALL TOGETHER

Starting with a backlit scene, I selected a dark marble effect surface to place my bowl on. The soup I am going to photograph is bright orange, so a neutral color will suit it best to make the color pop This board is a simple granite effect self-adhesive vinyl on a wooden board.

I diffused the light with some tracing paper taped to the window, placed my surface right up close and roughly set up two pieces of foam board to act as reflectors.

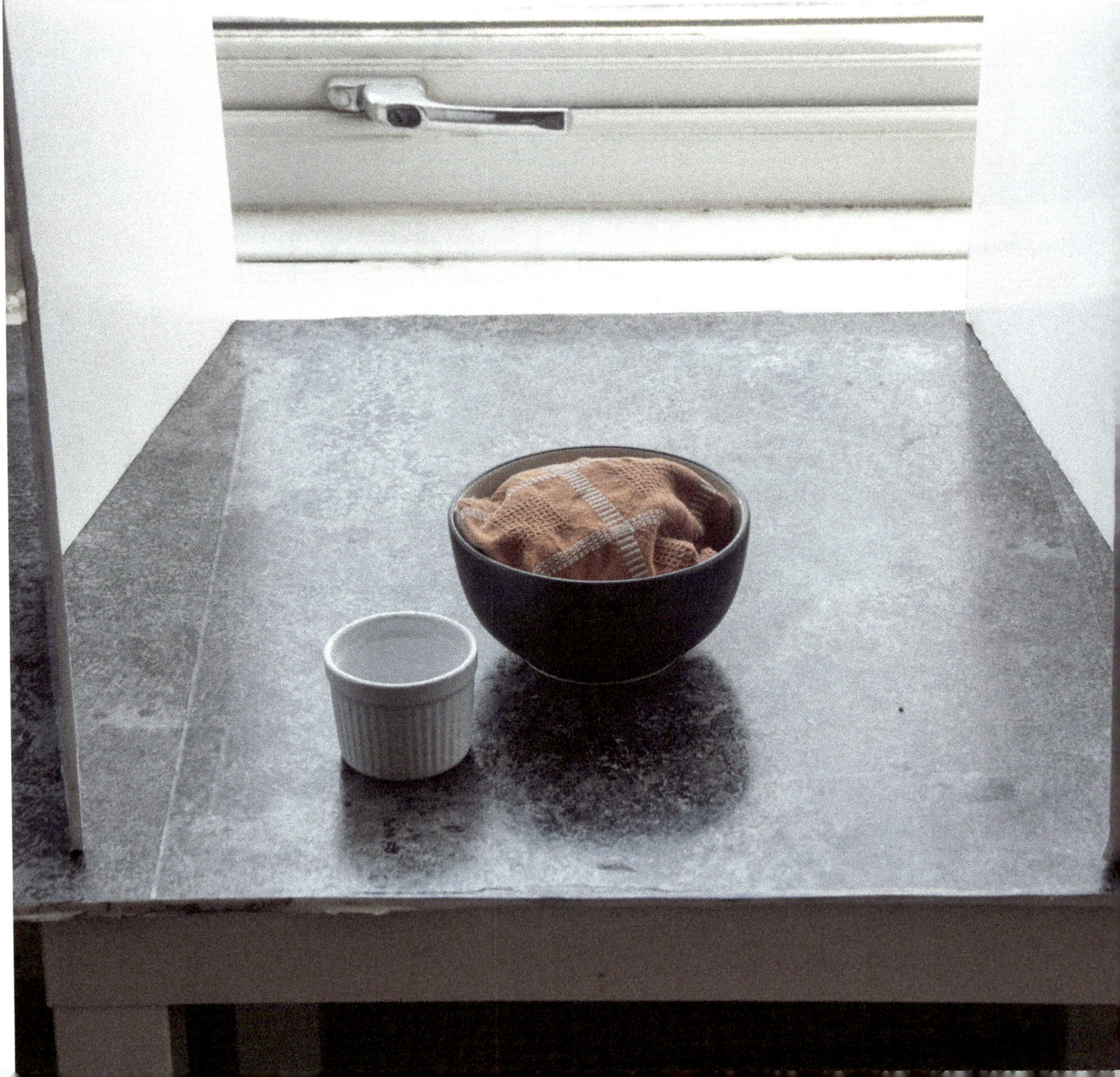

I have selected a black bowl for this soup because I don't want the viewer's attention distracted, placing a white or colored bowl on an already dark surface will cause too much distraction.

I'm using this orange towel as a stand in for my soup. It's roughly the same tone.

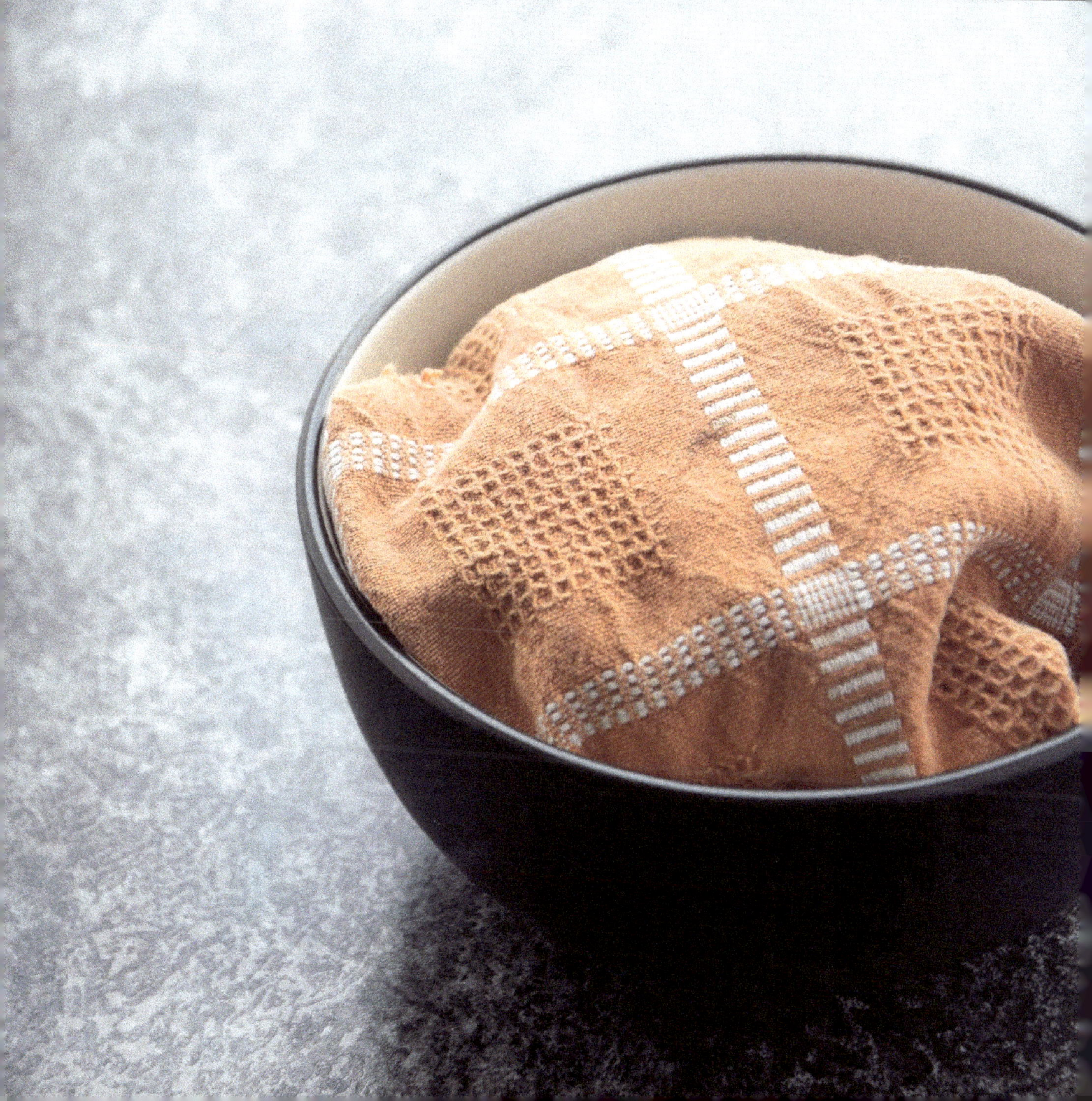

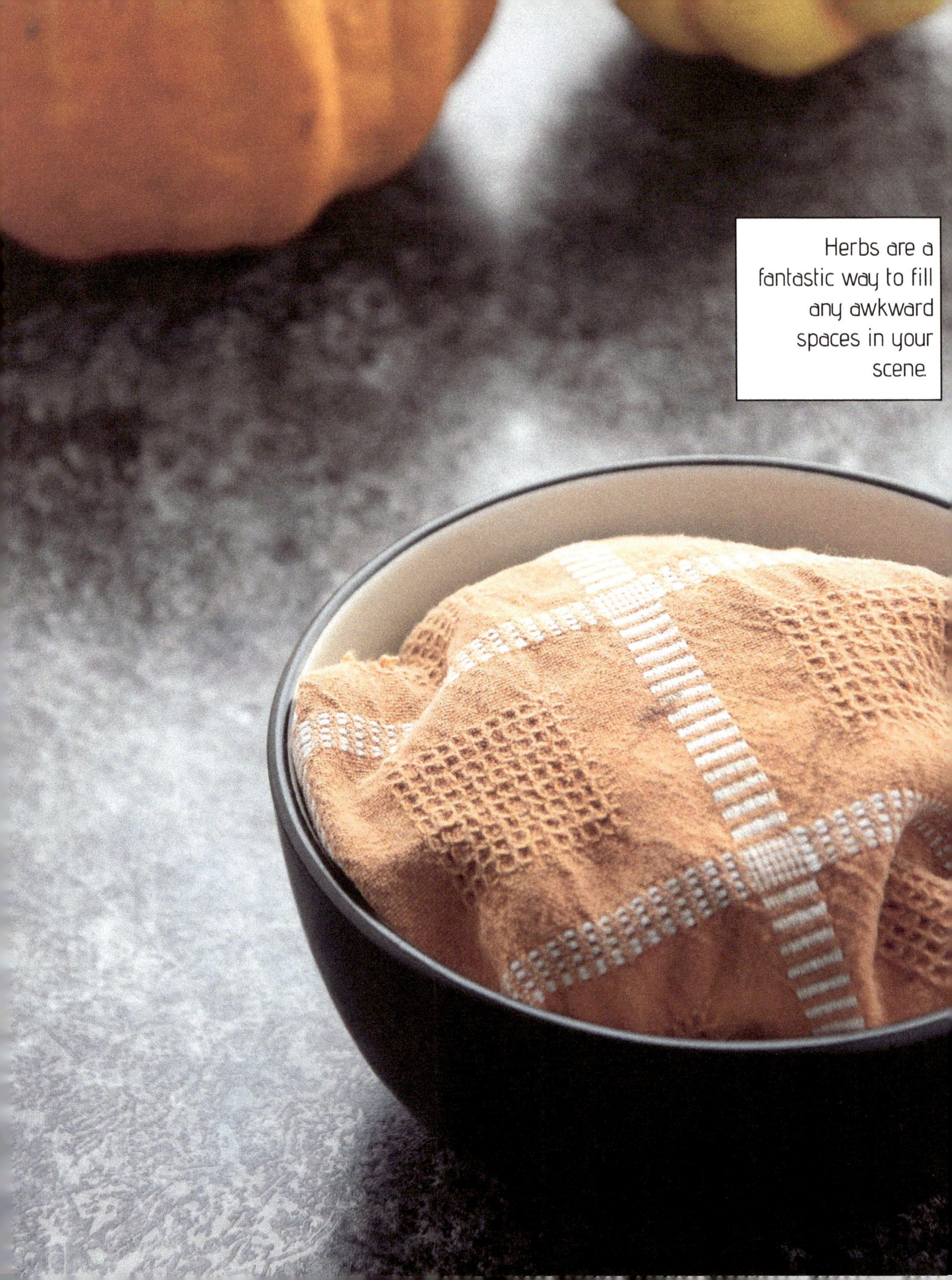

Herbs are a fantastic way to fill any awkward spaces in your scene.

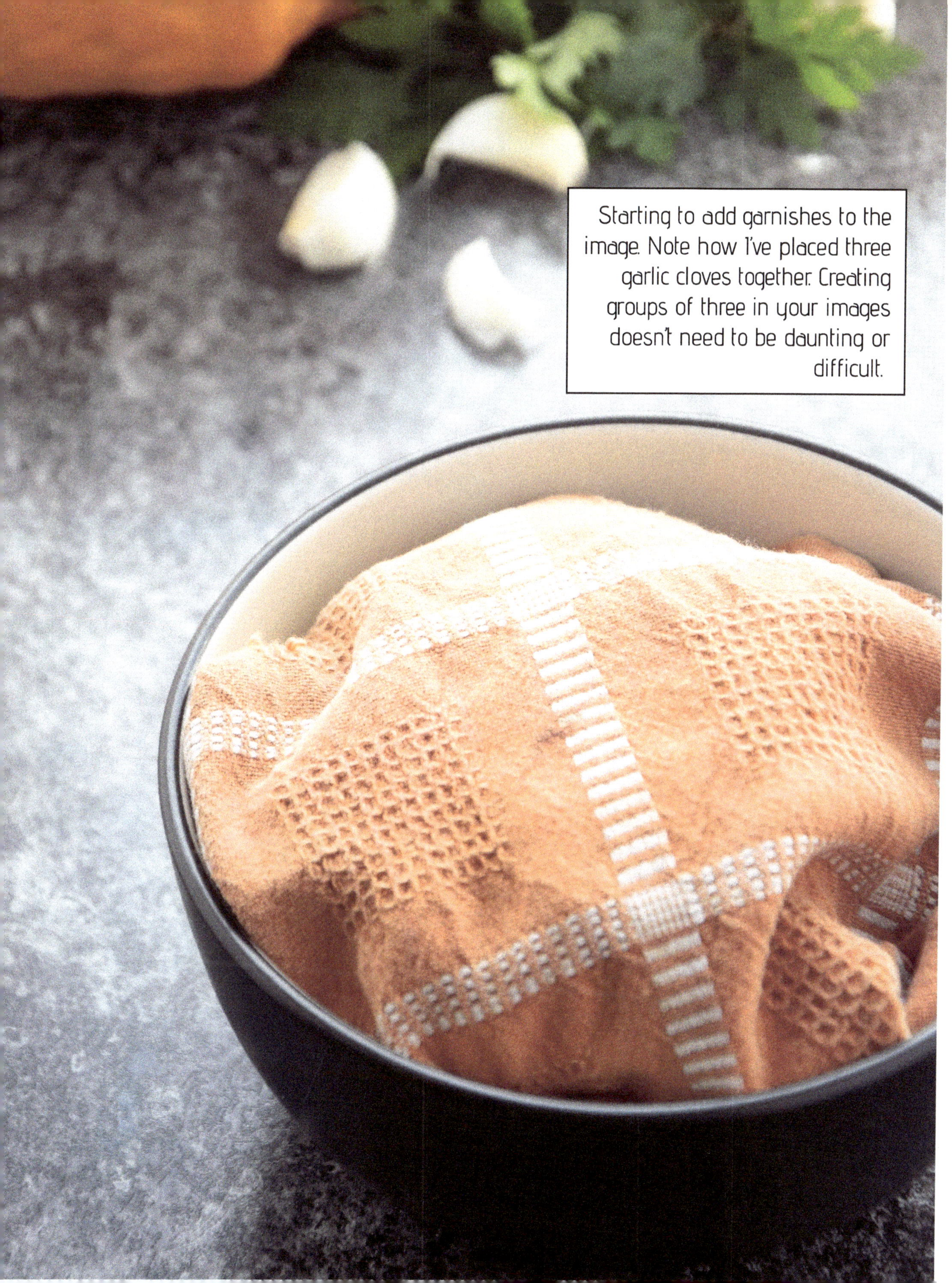

Starting to add garnishes to the image. Note how I've placed three garlic cloves together. Creating groups of three in your images doesn't need to be daunting or difficult.

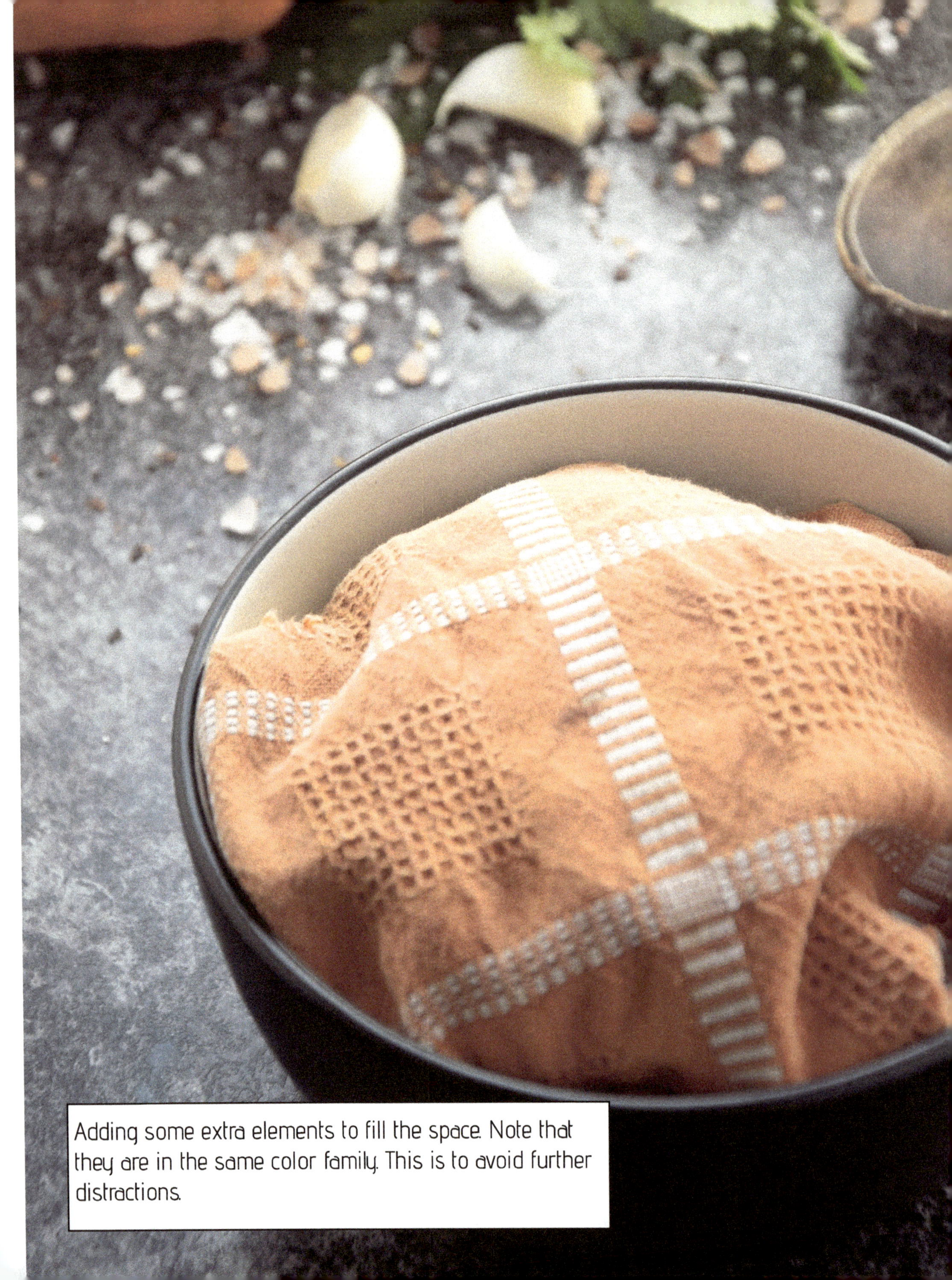

Adding some extra elements to fill the space. Note that they are in the same color family. This is to avoid further distractions.

Starting to think about those leading lines and extra elements that set the scene. Who has soup without a spoon?

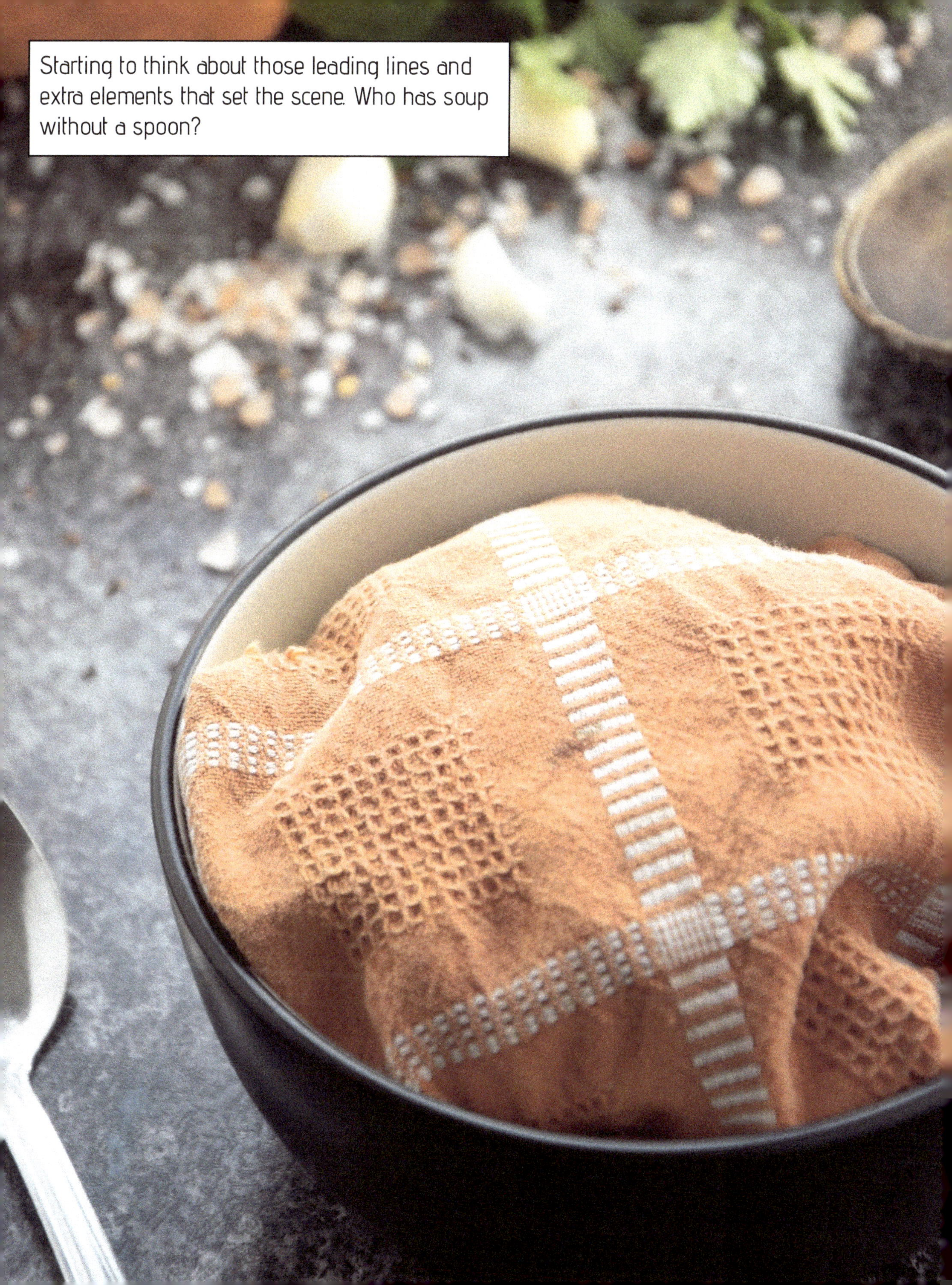

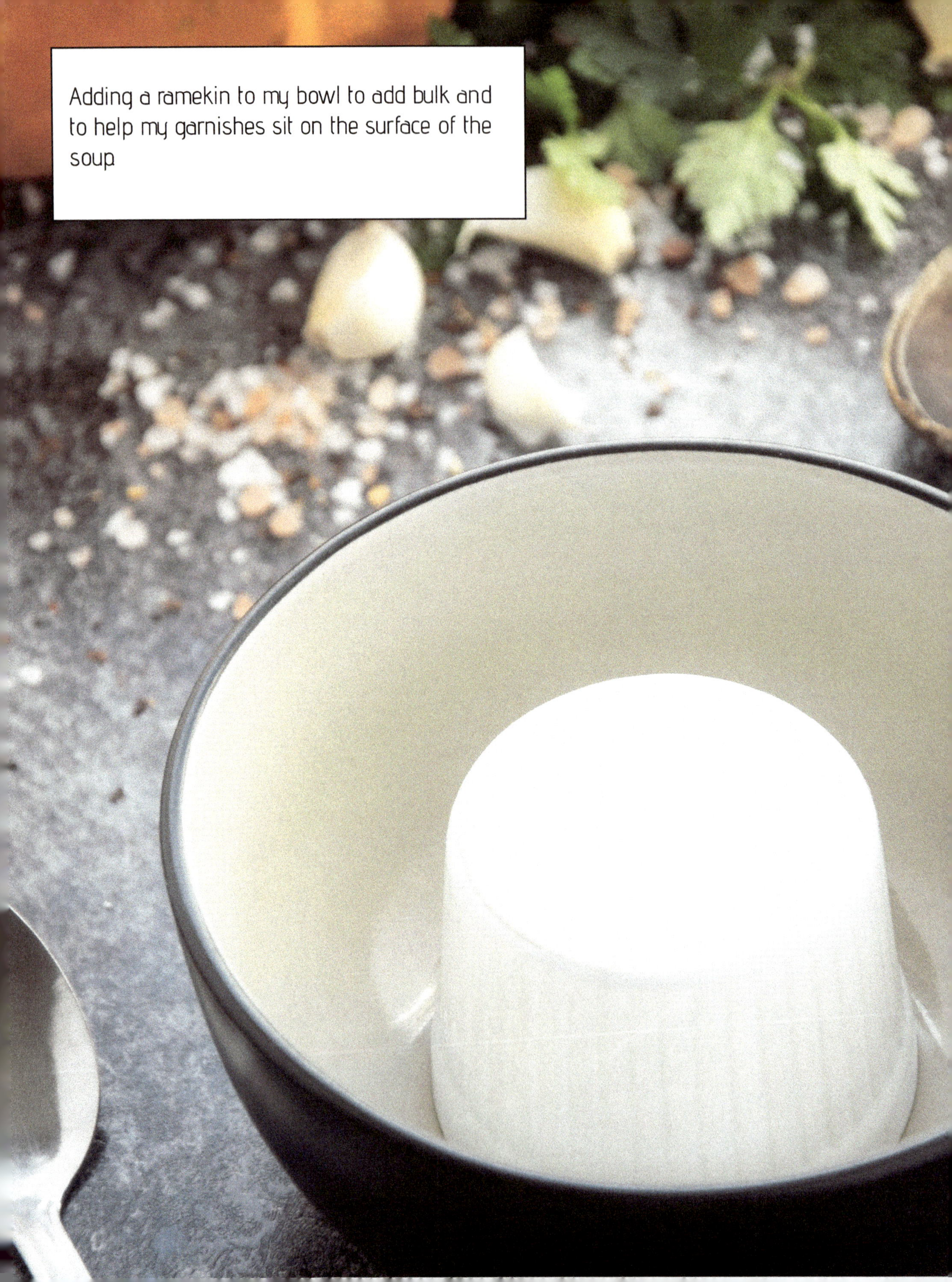

Adding a ramekin to my bowl to add bulk and to help my garnishes sit on the surface of the soup.

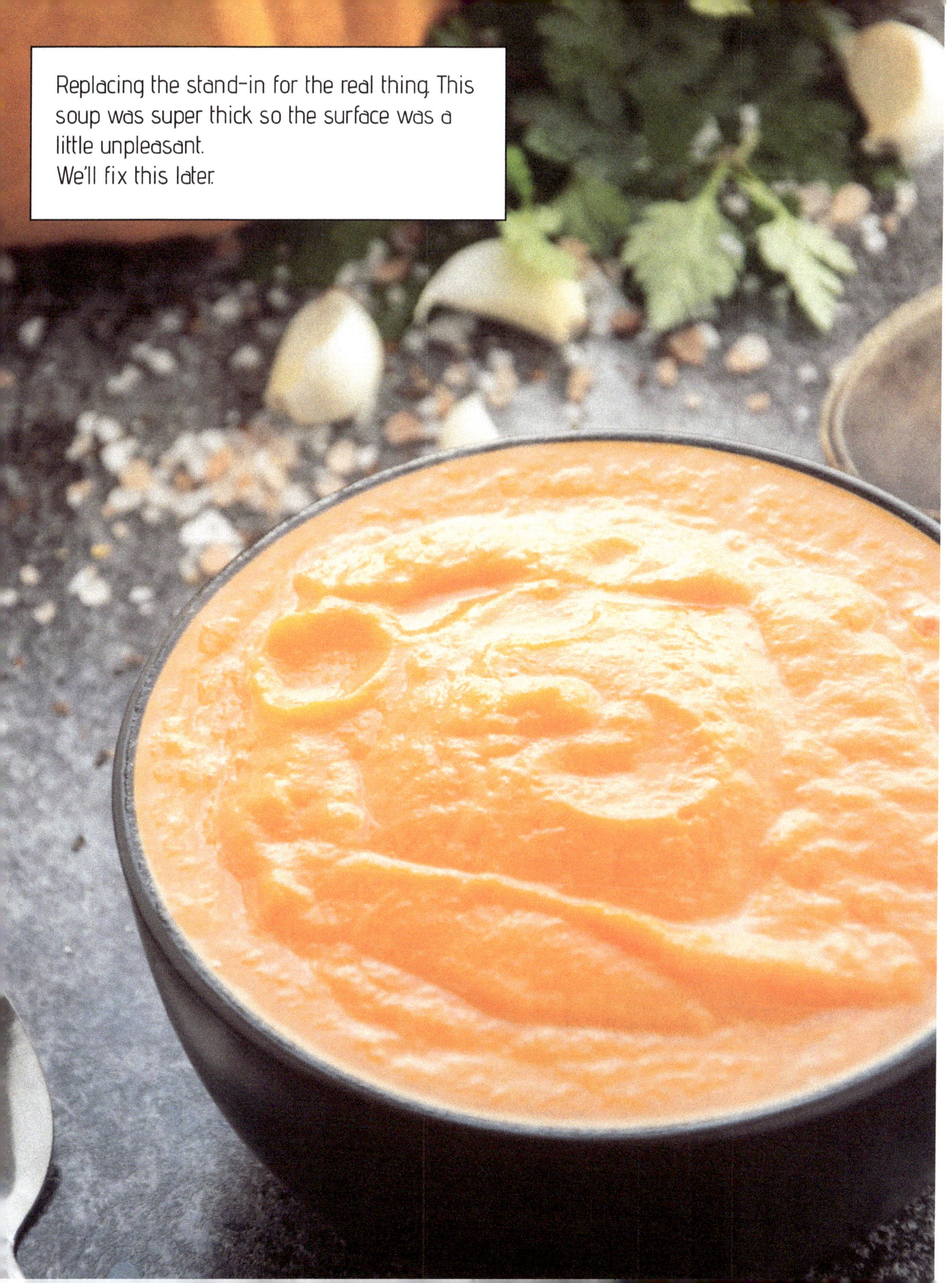

Replacing the stand-in for the real thing. This soup was super thick so the surface was a little unpleasant.
We'll fix this later.

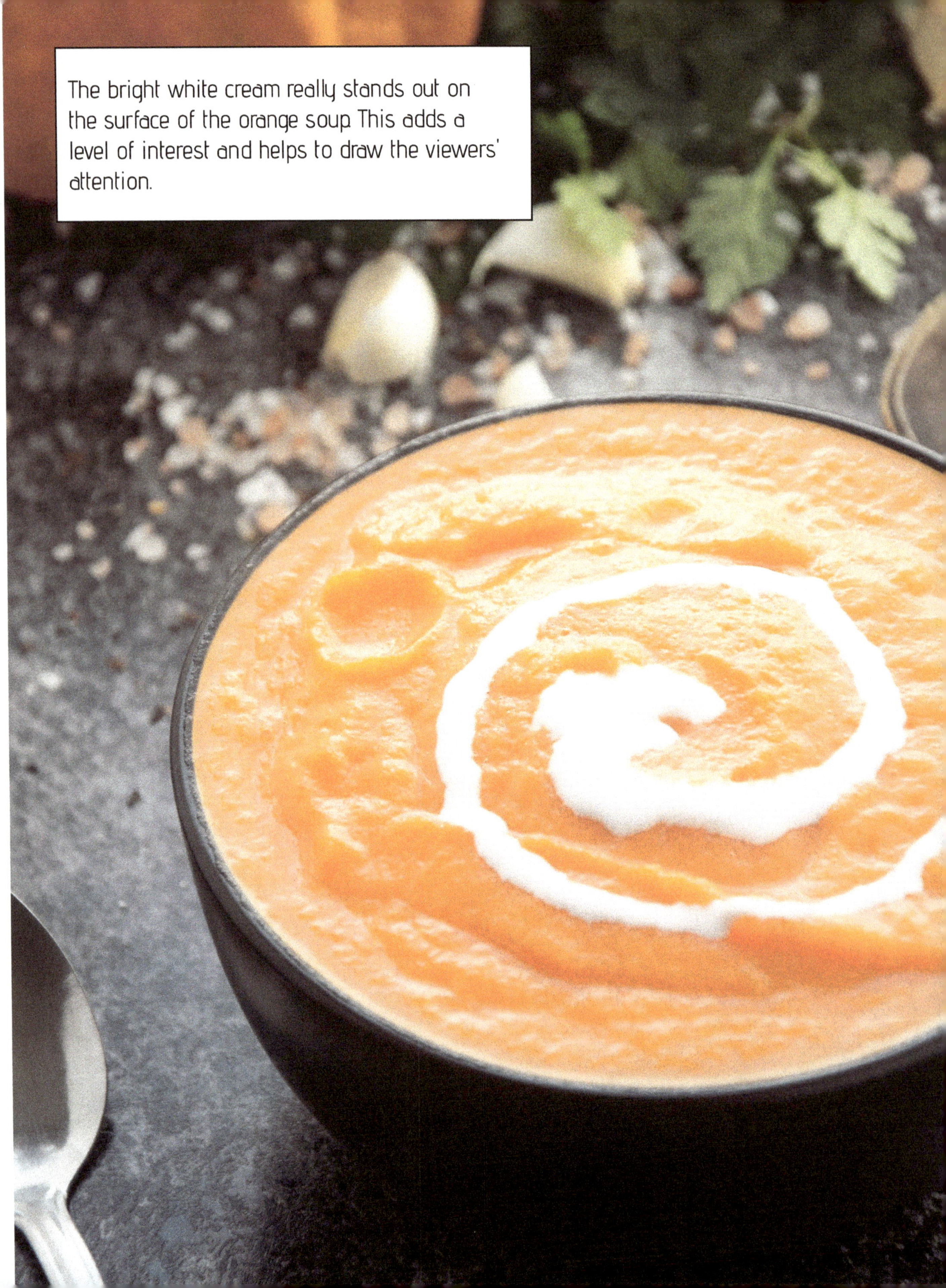

The bright white cream really stands out on the surface of the orange soup This adds a level of interest and helps to draw the viewers' attention.

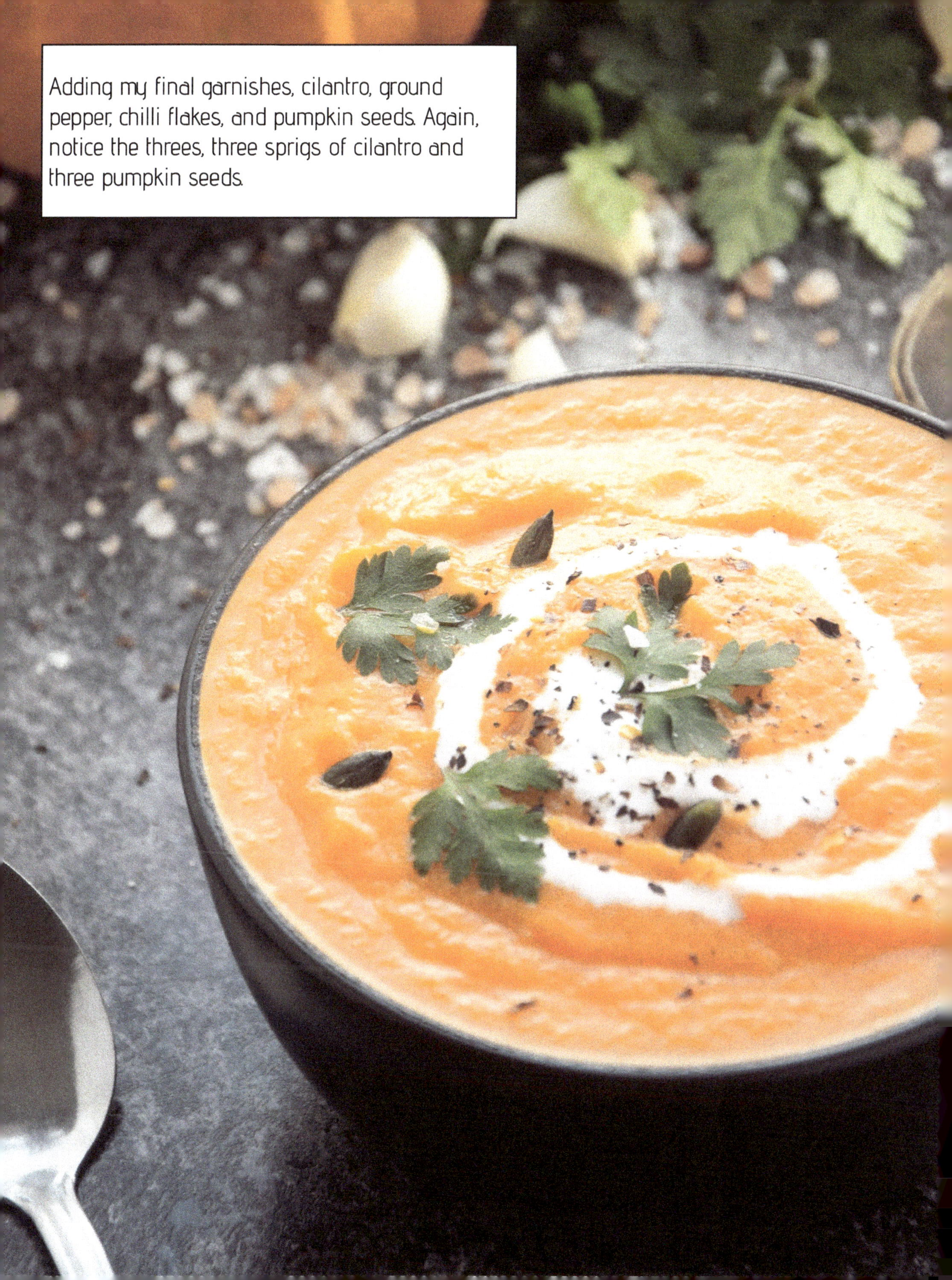

Adding my final garnishes, cilantro, ground pepper, chilli flakes, and pumpkin seeds. Again, notice the threes, three sprigs of cilantro and three pumpkin seeds.

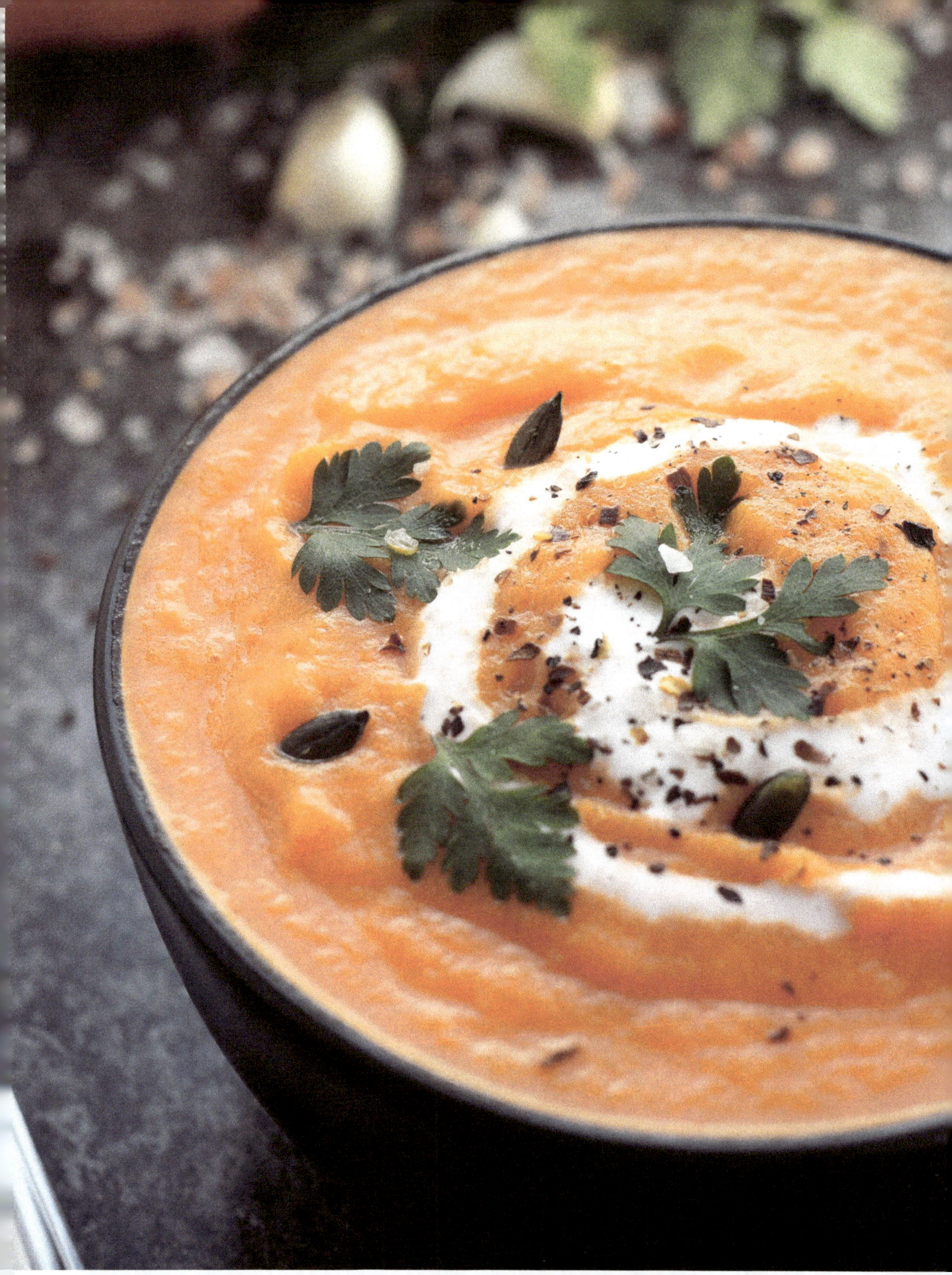

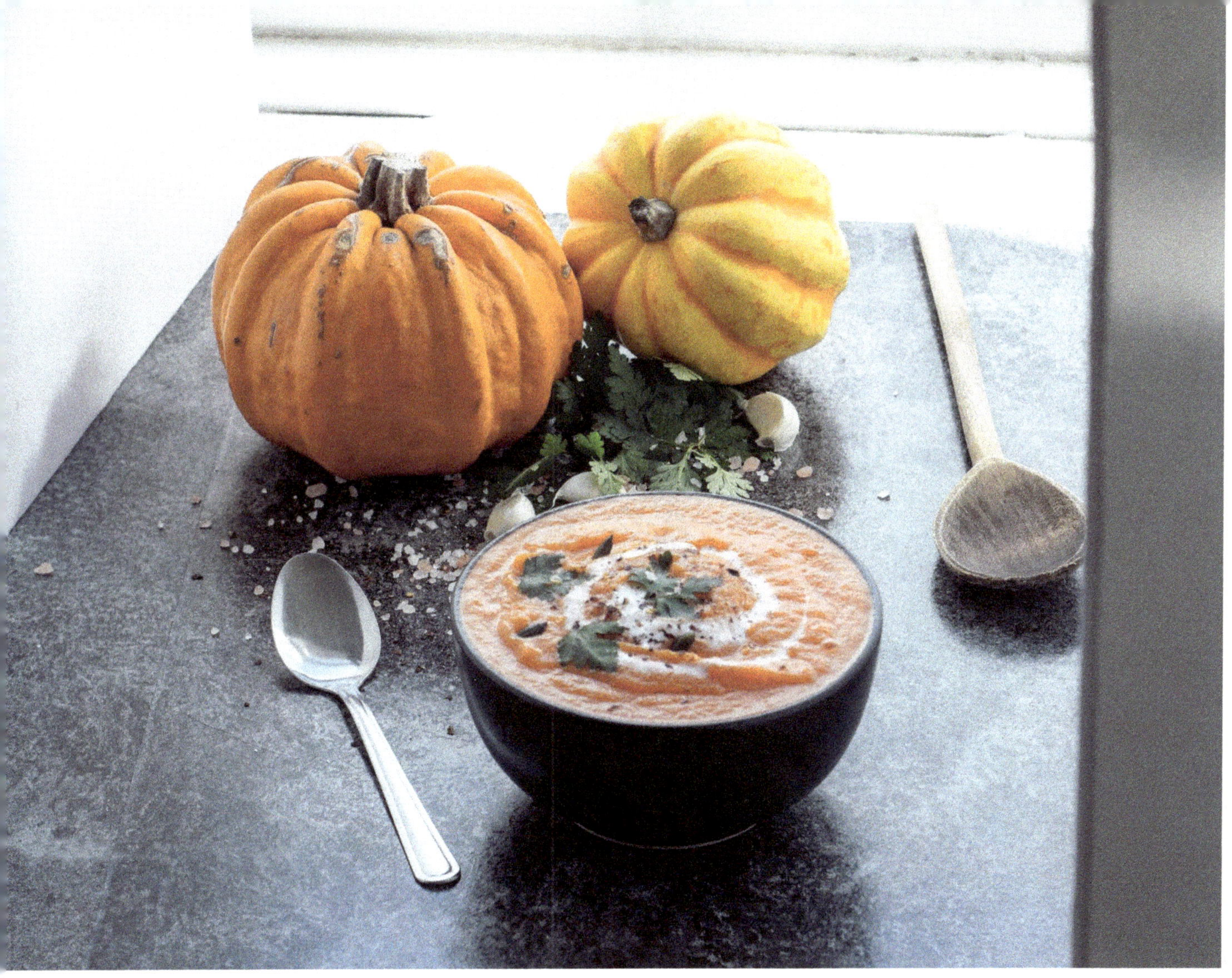

The final set up I played around a lot with the wooden spoon and in the end, it was just peeking in to fill some space. Sometimes, you don't need to see the whole object, just a portion of it is necessary to fill a little space.

When you have your final set up complete. You can take your shot safe in the knowledge that your image looks amazing. Once you have that shot, you can experiment moving the camera around, moving the props or even switching up lenses. Here I got in a little closer with a 50mm lens, set my aperture wide to blur the background even more and focused in on the garnish.

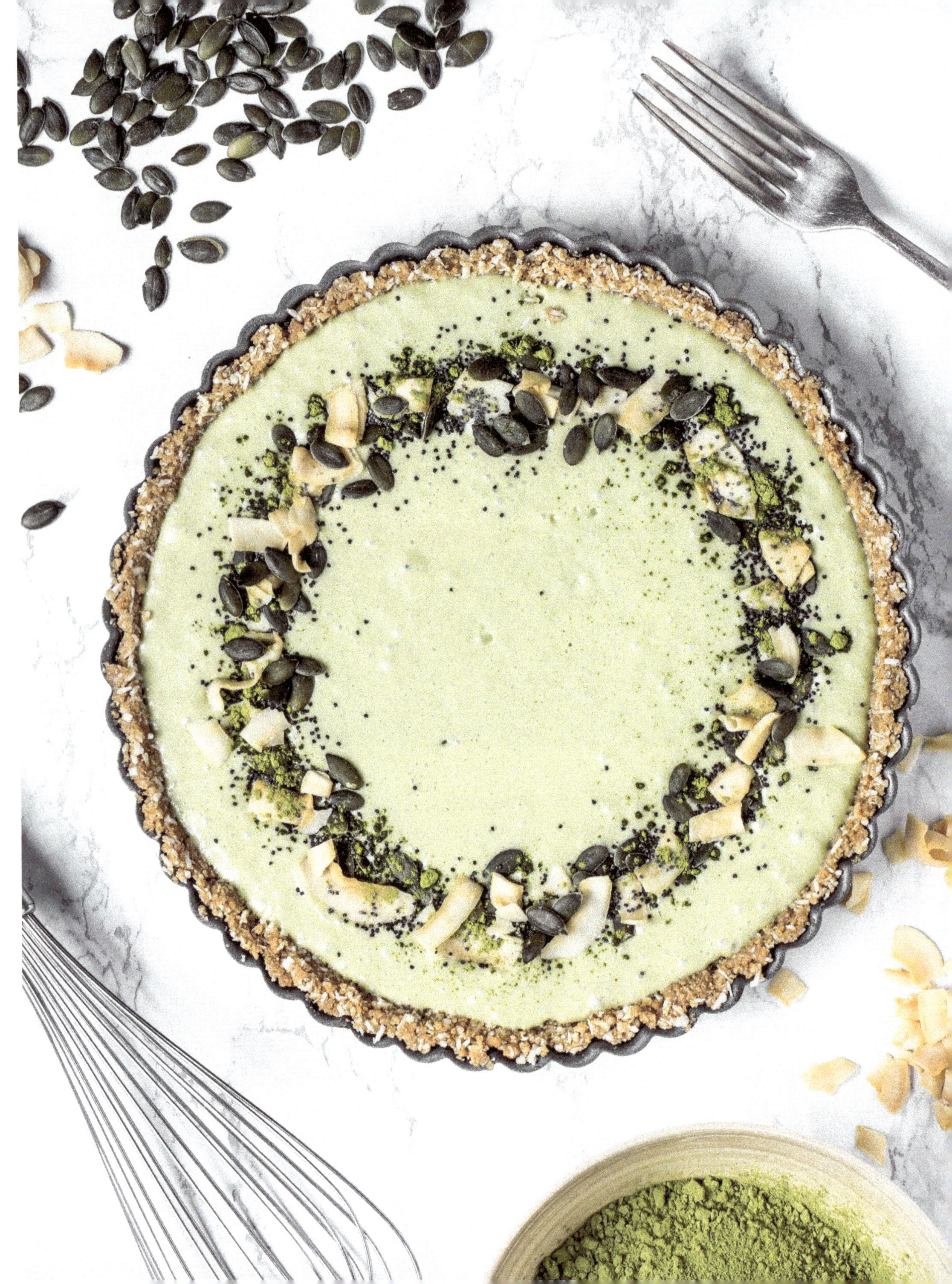

Conclusion

As photographers, it's important to remember the senses. Food is a sensual experience, we smell the beautiful aromas, we view the plate and see the colors, shapes, and textures. We even hear the food when it sizzles in the pan. When we taste it, we feel the texture with our mouths and we feel the temperature, is it hot or cold? As photographers, it's our job to capture that experience in a single image, we have to encapsulate that entire sensual experience using only sight.

Remember, if in doubt, keep things simple. Neutral plates, props, and backgrounds paired with beautiful light and delicious food are, sometimes all you need. Try not to overcomplicate things if you're unsure. Sometimes stripping everything back and concentrating on the dish can bring things into perspective.

Take the information in this book and experience it, try out every technique and see what works for you. It's important that you never stop learning, experimenting and creating. Photography techniques and trends are always evolving and so should you. Never, I repeat, never, stop growing as a photographer. Pour over other people's work constantly and immerse yourself in food photography culture. It's the only way you will stay on top of trends.

Most importantly of all, never lose your passion for food or food images. Find little inspirations every day. Visit farmers market and marvel at the beautiful produce. Visit new restaurants to find new food trends and find inspiration in the wealth of images available online. Never let yourself lose that passion and drive for making beautiful images. It's what makes you amazing!

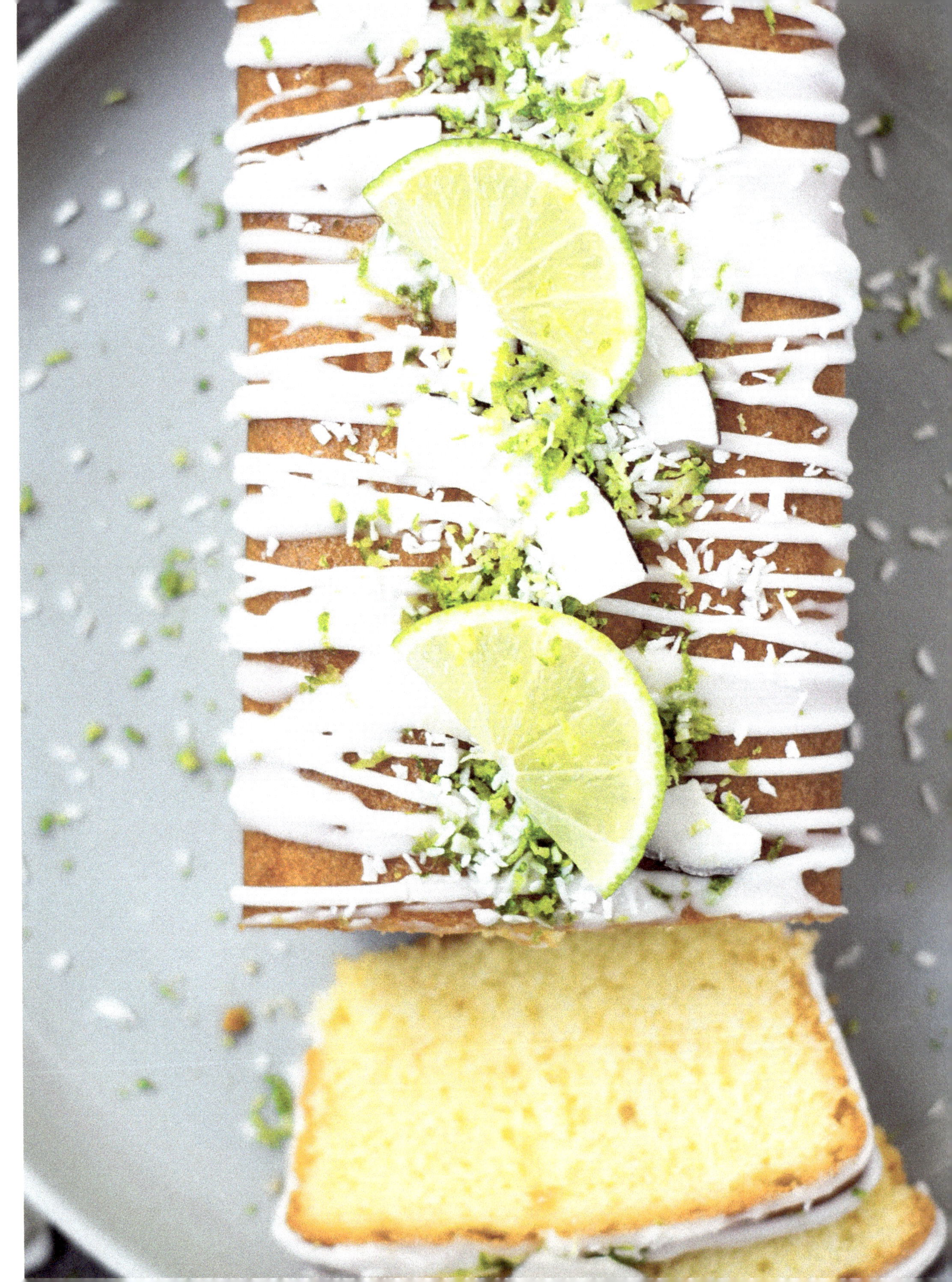

Lightning Source UK Ltd.
Milton Keynes UK
UKHW050335190620
365180UK00004B/54

9 780368 522413